FATHERING TOGETHER

D1598138

Aunt Annie,

Thanks fo' all the support !.!!

Peace

B. Joh.

FATHERING TOGETHER

LIVING A CONNECTED DAD LIFE

BRIAN ANDERSON

NEW DEGREE PRESS

FATHERING TOGETHER
Living a Connected Dad Life

ISBN   979-8-88504-541-4 *Paperback*
          979-8-88504-867-5 *Kindle Ebook*
          979-8-88504-657-2 *Ebook*

To my wife, Laura, for your eternal patience and care

To my daughters, Clara and Natalie, may your spirited energy never burn out.

CONTENTS

"We can honestly say that we are immortal. Not by the time that we will live, but by the wisdom that we will leave."

—BENJAMIN ROSS AIKEN, 1980–1996

INTRODUCTION

This book is a love letter to my fellow dads.

I'm going to go out on a limb and guess you don't say, "I love you" enough to your friends, let alone your partner and children. So let me start with it here.

I love you, Man!

Not because I know you, but because you've taken a leap to being a dad and with that leap comes a world of responsibilities none of us are prepared for even if we read every book and go to every prenatal appointment.

In this love letter to you, I'm laying out a challenge I hope you agree to pick up. This challenge is to reimagine fatherhood. It is one based on servant leadership and connection. And if you are reading this, it probably means one of two things: You're expecting a new baby, and you want to start off on the right foot. You're already a dad, and you're looking to repair and strengthen your relationship with your children.

In either case, I'm glad you are here, and I'm excited to journey through fatherhood together.

* * *

Here are a few things to know about me and Fathering Together (the organization) before you dive in:

First, I'm on this journey with you. At the time of publication, I've got an eight- and six-year-old. They are fierce, independent daughters who in one minute ask to cuddle and the next for a wrestling match.

They are the reason this book exists.

In early 2021, I began conceiving this book after a terrible conversation with my eight-year-old. I had been working a full-time job while trying to get Fathering Together off the ground. For over a year, in my spare time, I'd been building a community of dads. Despite what I told myself, the experience was all-consuming.

One night, as I tucked my daughter into bed, she had a frown on her face.

I asked, "What's up, Honey?"

She sighed and replied, "Dad, I know you are trying to help other dads to be good dads, but you aren't being a good dad to me."

Her words were daggers, and she had no clue how painful it was for me to hear that. But every word rang true. I focused my spare time on other dads, not my children.

I had been pouring myself into my work as a way to ignore the pandemic and stresses of life. I was pouring my positive energy away from my family, not toward. Worst of all, I was being a hypocrite.

Thankfully, my daughter's verbal slap woke me up. And since that day, I haven't been perfect, but I'm much more aware of how I'm using my energy to build stronger relationships within my family instead of giving them my leftovers.

Second, I'm never satisfied with the status quo. I'm always looking to improve the way I walk through life and the systems that provide for all of us to live better healthier lives. You may or may not agree with me on how to change those systems, and that's okay! Life is better when we have conflict and challenge. It forces us to think critically and see things from different angles. Many of my best friends who I've made through my dad communities don't share the same ideology, spirituality, skin color, or gender identity as me. We are all stronger for it.

One of my dear friends that I met through my Dads with Daughters Facebook group illustrates this perfectly. As the group began to expand, I posted a call for volunteers, and he responded. When I clicked on his avatar, a grim reaper riding a flaming Harley-Davidson motorcycle greeted me. I figured there was more to the story, so I reached out.

Over several late-night conversations, it was clear that his daughter had changed his life for the better, and he would do anything to ensure she had every opportunity in life. I wanted the same for my daughters, and our shared interest began a close friendship. As our conversations continued, I learned he's a libertarian, gun-owning motorcycle repairman who has served time and lives with severe disabilities. I also learned he homeschools his daughter, cares for his community through random acts of service, and runs addiction recovery groups for dads in the area.

We disagree on just about everything, but we're working together to find a better solution for our daughters.

So, to you, dear reader, you and I may never cross paths on the street. We'll probably disagree on a fair number of things. But I hope we can both agree that creating a world that welcomes our amazing, gifted, and talented children is a shared goal.

Third, speaking of Facebook, my co-founder Chris Lewis gets credit for starting Dads with Daughters on the platform and lighting a fire that began with fifty friends and is now one of the largest dad groups on the planet. As of this publication, our membership is at 126,000 dads and their posts, conversations, and calls for help fueled the creation of this book. These members, along with dozens of moms and people who aren't parents, helped me write this book. I may have typed on the keyboard, but through hundreds of interviews and late-night conversations, I found themes and trends from their personal stories and anecdotes.

These trends point to a new definition of fatherhood and a new way of being present for our children, our partners, and society. Sadly, it took a pandemic, millions of lost lives, and a fundamental shift in how dads see themselves and the responsibilities they hold.

WHERE WE ARE

In Part 1, I'll share my journey to fatherhood while highlighting how dads have traditionally been present in our society and how dads are shifting their role and responsibilities in the workplace and in the home. This shift has come as the archetypes that guided our dads and grandfathers have faltered. Most of them didn't have technology to find answers for everything. They had word of mouth and card catalogues (remember them?). They didn't have the means to connect instantly with experts when their kids were sick or misbehaving, or any number of other "anomalies" that make us question our parenting strategies.

Even if they did take the time to talk to experts, most were told to leave it up to their wives. Their place was earning a living and being the breadwinner while their wife raised the kids and managed the home. In this way, the "ideal" nuclear family served as the template for perfections. Yet, the nuclear family is far from ideal. David Brooks' 2020 article in *The Atlantic* tracks the disfunction that came with codifying family as one dad, one mom, and kids, but trends prior to the pandemic show a vast diversification in family structure with same-sex marriages, blended families, and multigenerational homes that are much more common throughout the world.

Another trend that took place during the pandemic was the departure of women from the workplace. Some journalists and researchers say workplaces look more like the 1960s than the 2010s. Not all women left the workforce. Most just picked up additional hours at home while dads didn't. Researchers and consultants like Eve Rodsky, Leslie Forde, Dan Carlson, and Richard Petts highlight how women are working more than ever before, yet men aren't picking up an equal share of household responsibilities.

Ironically, most dads want to be involved, they just don't know exactly how to do it. Too many messages have been ingrained in us to see ourselves as our job, as the product of what we provide for the economy and society. So if this is the case, let's meet dads where they are.

I'll lay out a new vision for fatherhood that is based in Robert Greenleaf's servant leadership model. In the 1960s, Robert Greenleaf wrote *The Servant as Leader* to revolutionize the corporate world. He believed a CEO couldn't be at their best without their staff being at their best; thus, it was the CEO's job to empower their staff and serve them so that all might thrive. Dozens of companies have turned around profit margins with this model. Former CEOs have written hundreds of books with reflections on their use of the model.

I found three blog posts connecting servant leadership to fatherhood.

This book is a love letter to my fellow dads because I believe in our capacity to change and our capacity to build a world where our children can thrive. If we aren't doing that, what's the point of making six figures or owning the largest house on the block?

WHERE WE ARE GOING

In Section 2 I'll lay out a pathway for this new vision by diving into the various components of servant leadership and how dads are living out aspects of Greenleaf's model. Greenleaf's article outlines dozens of aspects of being the perfect servant leader. No one person has the ability to do all of them. So I've chosen ten characteristics that fall into four areas: Communication, Other-Oriented, Advocacy, and Community. Focusing on these areas will cultivate a dad-first mindset.

No one dad that I interviewed had every skill. I definitely don't. But we come to fatherhood with preexisting strengths, so I've written this book to be used as you need it. If you already have strong communication skills, skip chapter eight. If you need help to be more emotionally expressive, don't skip chapter seven.

If you're struggling to understand your child's gifts and talents, I recommend chapter nine. If you want to be a stronger advocate for your child, check out chapters eleven and twelve. And I recommend that all of us read chapter thirteen. As the title implies, fatherhood is not a solo journey. Our children will constantly outsmart us and no one dad has everything it takes to be perfect. So find a community, lean on that community for support, and give back when you see someone in need.

WHO IS THIS BOOK FOR?

I want to be clear that I'm writing this book for dads who live in the United States, or at least Western cultures, who have full-time jobs (or grew up believing they had to have one to secure their manhood), and are struggling to build emotional connections with their family. These are the dads who are stuck in a mindset that isn't benefiting them, their families, or society.

What it does is lead to alienation and disconnection.

As my daughter reminded me over a year ago, I was killing myself with busyness and not productivity. I was alienating myself from her when she needed me the most. Over the last eighteen months, I've reimagined my fatherhood and my life to have a dad-first mindset, and I invite you to do the same.

Our children and our partners deserve more from us than just a paycheck. So join me as we reimagine fatherhood together.

PART 1

FATHERHOOD AS I KNOW IT

1

MY JOURNEY TO FATHERHOOD

"I'm a father; that's what matters most. Nothing matters more."

—GORDON BROWN

We are led to believe that fatherhood begins with a gasp and a cry. As we meet our child and hold them for the first time in our hands, we become dads. But, in reality, being a dad shouldn't start when we hold our children. It needs to start much, much earlier.

Fatherhood is like a marathon. You don't just walk out your front door and run 26.2 miles. If you did, you'd end up with the poor Spartan who ran the first one (hint: he died). Marathons take months of training and preparation.

Fatherhood should too.

I would like to think my fatherhood journey began when I was sixteen. I had a job at my local library reshelving books. I was in the youth room, a dreaded assignment because little kids rarely keep books in order, and they are everywhere!

As I knelt to put picture books back into place, I heard a little boy call to his dad. Something about his voice and the way he said, "daddy" sparked something within me. I heard a voice in my own head say, "This is who you will become someday."

Thankfully, I was just mature enough to wait. But I did put little into becoming a dad while I waited. I didn't read any books on parenthood. I babysat for a few families in the neighborhood but understanding the full weight of fatherhood was something no one expected of me.

Then, in the spring of 2013, my wife handed me a card at breakfast. I knew before I opened it that we were expecting.

"Seriously?" I asked between tears.

"Yes, she'll be here in December," Laura responded through tears of her own.

Even with a seven-month deadline, I procrastinated. I read a few books. I built a crib and a dresser. I joined my wife on a trip to Buy Buy Baby and helped my wife pick out all the things one might expect, but the balance of preparation definitely leaned toward my wife.

Then, on December 12, 2013, everything changed.

I was at an interfaith gathering in downtown Chicago. My friend was moderating the event and as the panel wrapped up and we broke for dinner, my phone vibrated.

My wife texted, "No need to rush home, but I think I'm in labor."

I walked up to my friend, showed him the text with a big grin, and hurried out the door.

Roughly thirty-two hours later, my daughter came into the world.

"There's the culprit!" The doctor exclaimed as she lifted our baby. She pulled the umbilical cord away from my daughter's neck, and my daughter's cries magnified one hundredfold. The thin cord had caused my daughter's heart rate to drop to alarming levels every time my wife's contractions got intense. Each time this happened, doctors and nurses would rush in, sedate my wife to slow the contractions, and the entire labor process would start all over again.

Thankfully, my daughter was alive and well. Her APGAR test confirmed everything was in the right place. And she was soon resting and breastfeeding.

We spent two days in the hospital until they discharged us. I still remember driving entirely too slowly as my wife and child sat in the back. Then, when we got into our house, I placed the baby carrier on the floor in the living room and stared at her.

Now what? No nurses. Just us.

"Can we leave her in there a bit longer?" my wife asked.

"I'm afraid to take her out," I replied.

Thus, life post-hospital for my family began.

Except it didn't. She was slightly jaundiced, and the doctor was concerned about her bilirubin levels.

Jaundice babies are not uncommon. Over 50 percent of babies fall within range of the diagnosis, where high levels of bilirubin remain in our body. Bilirubin is the scientific term for the stuff that remains after our red blood cells break down. Usually our livers process this quickly, but if a baby's liver is not fully functioning, the liver doesn't break it down fast enough, and their skin can take on a yellow hue. If the levels are too high, brain damage can occur, so doctors place babies under special lights in the neonatal unit to help speed up the bilirubin's decomposition.

Sometimes exposure to the sun can help expedite things, but December isn't known for ample sunlight in Chicago, so every day for the following week, we returned to the hospital for bloodwork. This meant I held my baby while she screamed as needles bit into her tiny feet.

After a week, the doctors gave us the clear. My wife and I set to work being parents and managing life with a third person in our house. We'd been talking about it in theory, but theory and practice are two very different things.

In theory, our baby would never blowout her diaper and sleep through the night. In practice, we battled explosive diapers, sleepless nights, and more. Thankfully, my wife had dozens of mom groups with whom she connected. Both online in virtual communities and with local stroller meetups, my wife met new friends and forged ahead into motherhood.

I looked for dad groups and found none that made sense to me.

Most of the dad groups were meant for dads with kids in school, not newborns. Others upheld gendered roles that my wife and I swore against. I wanted a group to help me normalize my experiences and learn strategies that would help me support my wife and our baby.

So I set about creating one.

THE BIRTH OF FATHERING TOGETHER

Fathering Together began as a storytelling night. For a few months, my dad, friends, and I would meet at a local taproom and swap stories. Eventually, I convinced them we should do an open mic night and tell our fatherhood stories to an audience.

Some were excited. Others reluctantly agreed.

At our first of two storytelling nights, we had six dads share a story. The first dad shared his experiences fostering children before his wife miraculously got pregnant.

Then, within days of their son's birth, their former foster child died of a rare form of cancer. We were left speechless, but the night went on.

Another shared how a nurse thrust papers into his hands, asking, "If something goes wrong, who do we save?" His wife had just been wheeled into the operating room for an emergency C-Section, which is never a part of a birth plan, but here he was standing in the hallway of a hospital signing documents and trying to comprehend what this nurse was actually saying to him. He's now the proud father of three rambunctious boys.

Then my neighbor stepped up to share his story. He hadn't planned on sharing but came to support me and my hairbrained idea for a storytelling night.

He began, "I never met my father. In fact, I didn't know he existed until I was thirty, and my mom told me she kept his identity from me." The room got very quiet. Everyone else in the room had a father growing up. My neighbor was sharing a story that none of us could relate to, but all of us feared.

"So I set out to try and find him. Turns out, I have a halfbrother. When I found him, I learned my father died a month earlier." My neighbor paused for a while. Then he continued to share how his father had never known he had a son. My neighbor's mom and his father had had a fling and so she hadn't contacted him. He went on to share how he and his half-brother became good friends through the entire thing.

Then he paused again and concluded, "I'm still figuring out how to be a dad because I never had one. But I know one thing is true. My kids will never not know how much I love them."

When my neighbor finished, no one else took to the stage. Everyone clapped and celebrated the night. The next storytelling night was in collaboration with a local arts foundation, and despite ambitions for more, I had to put a pause on the storytelling because Fathering Together would shift abruptly with the success of another fatherhood project I was associated with.

I met Dr. Christopher Lewis through a professional association for higher education. I had volunteered to organize a men and masculinities conference for the Midwest region and Dr. Christopher Lewis was my contact at the association to make sure the event was a success.

Five years later, he sent me an invitation to a Facebook group he called Dads with Daughters: We're All on a Journey of Discovery.

About fifty dads answered Chris's call, and I scrolled through my friend list and sent invitations out to them, too. This was in February 2018. Within a month, we'd climbed to 500 members, and I asked Chris if he wanted help moderating the group based on my past experiences. I'm not sure he knew what he was getting into when he said yes. Because I immediately started creating a plan to strengthen the culture, set up guidelines for posts, and began asking questions of the dads in the group.

By October 2018, we had 2,500 members. A year later, in March 2019, we crossed 10,000 members. Chris and I couldn't believe it. Then we got a message asking if we wanted to be part of the #MoreTogether campaign that Facebook launched that summer. At first, we thought we were being scammed. Someone wanted to spotlight our little community?

But we said yes and right after Mother's Day, I got a call from my mom asking if I had seen this commercial with two dads going to a baseball game and commenting to each other on Facebook about it. I hadn't, but a few weeks later, I was at the movies with one of my neighbors and the commercial came on before the movie. It was surreal.

Our numbers started climbing rapidly after that and we put out a call for volunteers to help us meet the demand. Some of those first volunteers are still with us helping support dads, and we were all amazed when the commercial ran during the opening football game of the 2019–2020 season. In the span of four hours, we had over 3,000 new member requests.

That fall, we recruited a handful of friends to help us form a board for Fathering Together and we built a plan. By the time 2019 concluded, we had surpassed 100,000 members and would eventually level off around 126,000 dads representing nearly every corner of the globe with faith traditions, political views, and family situations as diverse as you would expect.

This diversity made me and my leadership team stronger and led to the concepts that follow in this book. Dads from all walks of life helped inform my fatherhood practice just as much as I helped inform theirs. Through long conversations, challenging disagreements, and emotional cries for help, it became clear a new approach to fatherhood was essential for our society. But to create a new approach to fatherhood, one that is centered in servant leadership, I had to understand where fatherhood came from so we wouldn't repeat the same mistakes.

2

WHO DADS HAVE BEEN

*"I define fatherhood as a summation of all the biological aspects
and being a dad is a summation of all the emotional connections you build."*

—ROSS A.

HISTORY OF FATHERHOOD

Being a father (someone who provides sperm to an egg)
is hardly a given in our culture today and being a good
dad (someone who is actively engaged in raising their
child) can be even more challenging. Many of the dads
I spoke with often referenced how emotionally distant
their dads were for them. One even shared that the only
time his father was present was during sporting events
or musical productions. He was never present at meals or
just to talk. This led the interviewee to believe the only
way to win his father's affection was through his actions.
He had to earn his father's love.

So I began wondering what it would take to be emotionally present and connected to our children and why it was so challenging.

I'm not alone in wondering about these connections and challenges. In recent years, researchers and historians have been evaluating the role of fathers, and men, in Western societies. Michael A. G. Haykin makes note that "over the past two centuries, there has been a steady recession of the social role of fatherhood. Fathers have either gradually moved or been moved from the heart to the margins of family life." This coincides with the Industrial Revolution when work and family life were separated by physical location. For example, as more and more fathers left their farms to work in factories, the time they spent with their families diminished and relationships weakened, too.

Lawrence R. Samuel's book, *American Fatherhood*, focused on the latter half of the nineteenth century. A labor of love that came out of becoming a father later in life, he tracked the "new fatherhood movement." He writes, "Until the 1970s, men's role in family life was consistently underestimated, limited primarily to financial provider, no-nonsense disciplinarian, and occasional playmate." In other words, fathers became only breadwinners, while society expected mothers to be in charge of the emotional and social upbringing of the children.

As Samuel chronicles, the new fatherhood movement spanned the 1970s and 1980s, creating opportunities for dads to lean into their caring side and be present to their families in new ways. Statistics show an increase in at-home dads during this period, and dads taking more time to be involved with their partner's pregnancy and their child's early life.

On a recent trip to Chicago's Field Museum, the history of fatherhood played out in a new light. My children had been dying to see Sue, the most complete skeleton of a Tyrannosaurus Rex ever found. They'd been on a dinosaur kick, and I expected to spend much of our time in the exhibit. But five minutes later, they moved on. So we scoured the entire museum checking out Tsavo lions, ancient civilizations, and taking in an IMAX movie.

As we walked through the Ancient Americas section, something caught my attention. The dioramas often display men as the hunters who go out and hunted the mastodons and mammoths only to bring meat home to their families. They are posed with spears about to be hurled and carried scars with pride, but never do these dioramas display fathers carrying babies or helping with their families. Only the women in the diorama showcased care.

Yet, there is archaeological evidence to show that men were involved with caregiving. So why don't these dioramas depict that? Perhaps because we evolved from nomadic tribes into settled agricultural society, something shifted. Patriarchal structures formed with men using force to maintain structure and order.

THE AMBIGUOUS ROLE OF FATHERS

In describing the origins of fatherhood, Sebastian Krae-mer, child and adolescent psychiatrist, noted that father-hood developed out of a need for men to assert their place in society. With societal roles diversifying and hunter jobs giving way to administrative jobs, fathers had to make a case for their existence.

My friend and colleague, Dr. Bruce Linton, has led hun-dreds of group sessions for fathers over the last three decades and would agree with Kraemer. In his book *Fatherhood*, he points out that no definition of father-hood exists across time and cultures. Each has invented fatherhood to suit the needs and the experiences of the group. This creates an opportunity and a challenge because if fatherhood is malleable to the situation, why did it become so divorced from family structures? In con-trast to this, motherhood roles have always been clearly defined and linked directly to their biological necessity.

Michaeleen Doucleff has one suggestion. In her book *Hunt, Gather, Parent,* she examines what ancient cultures have done to raise empowered children, or as she puts it, "little humans." One clear distinction she makes is that in the recent history of the United States, we've created the nuclear family. This unit developed out of a post-World War II mindset where fathers worked, mothers stayed home, and kids went to school. If you've ever seen *Edward Scissorhands,* it offers a sardonic take on the cookie-cutter culture that developed with every house, car, and lawn looking identical. Pete Seeger's song, "Little Boxes," offers an even more cynical take.

What causes Michaeleen the biggest concern is not the cookie-cutter image, but the separation of parents from their previous generations. And as we've seen through this pandemic, parents are struggling to be everything for their children. Without grandparents present in the home, parents have had to be educators, cooks, housekeepers, and work too. Loading all of this onto their shoulders has led to massive burnout and employees leaving their jobs in what is being dubbed the Great Resignation.

Yet, prior to COVID-19's arrival, family dynamics were shifting away from the nuclear family. Blended families due to divorce and children out of wedlock, same-sex marriages, adoptions, and the rise in elder care were all influencing a shift from the ubiquitous nuclear family.

In recent years, a plethora of fatherhood-oriented groups have arisen alongside my own to help support fathers in their journey.

In 2003, three stay-at-home dads organized the first national non-profit organization to support dads who remained at home for their kids. Since then, the National At-Home Dad Network (NAHDN) has held annual conferences to gather dads together and build a community with a local campaign reminding all of us that "dads don't babysit."

NAHDN is relatively small, but pre-COVID statistics showed just how many couples were choosing the father to remain at home. According to the 2010 US Census, 32 percent of married fathers (approximately seven million dads) are "a regular source of care for their children under age fifteen, up from 26 percent from 2002." They define "regular care of children" as an arrangement that is consistent at least one day per week.

Unfortunately, data isn't out from 2020, and given the impact of COVID-19, data will remain unclear. The most recent numbers from the Pew Research Center share that in 2016, dads made up 17 percent of all stay-at-home parents up from 10 percent in 1989. Pew uses a broader definition that counts children under the age of eighteen and who have not worked for pay in the prior year, regardless of reason.

VIOLENCE AND GREED

What we know about the pandemic is that it is reverting many family dynamics over thirty years. And the gains in employment in late 2021 and early 2022 have primarily benefited men. Thus, the gendered lines are still very clear.

In reading bell hooks' *The Will to Change*, I'm reminded that change takes time and big change happens in bursts. In her letter to men, she points out the patriarchal system in which our society functions "has denied males access to full emotional well-being, which is not the same as feeling rewarded, successful, or powerful because of one's capacity to assert control over others." Yet, repeatedly, men equate their success at work as integral to their identity. So it stands to reason that they be the first to return to work while their wives stay home.

What I find more tragic is how inextricably linked fatherhood to masculinity and how inextricably linked masculinity is to violence and greed. Violent men are seen throughout history from Alexander the Great to Stalin from the Crusades to modern wars over small pieces of land. These have all been led by men whose sense of self-worth is wrapped up in how much land they control and how many people bow to their authority. In American history, you have men committing acts of violence to achieve a manifested destiny of western expansion and displacing thousands of people in the process too. While many are portrayed as heroes and defenders of freedom and honor by some, others see their acts as violent and genocidal.

In terms of greed, you have men like Rockefeller and Carnegie whose ambition garnered both to be the richest men in the United States. In later life they would create what we know as modern philanthropy, but to get there Rockefeller saw his company dismantled by the Supreme Court and Carnegie's legacy was marred by the Johnstown flood of 1889 that killed over two thousand people and the 1892 Homestead Strike that left ten dead and hundreds injured.

These men were also fathers. Their children have gone on to do great things with the wealth both accrued and their names common place within our cultural and educational institutions. But what about the average worker who struggles to make ends meet? What impact have all the fathers, who do not have common place names, but worked long hours to accumulate wealth, had on their children?

WHY FATHERHOOD MATTERS TO ME

My paternal grandfather passed away when I was sixteen. He was a working-class carpenter with six kids (five girls, one boy) who I remember as a real-life Marlboro man. All my memories revolved around four things:

- His house reeked of cigarettes.
- He always wore a plaid shirt, denim jeans, and bolo tie.
- He owned every Louie L'amour novel and read and re-read them every day.
- He was a carpenter everyone in town knew.

At his funeral, the priest pointed out that everyone knew Guy Anderson was coming because of his 1960s brown GMC truck with a faded stripe along the side. It finally died a few years before him.

My grandfather wasn't a horrible person, just not a great dad. He did what society expected of him. He made money and left the family stuff to his wife, my grand-mother, who died when I was two years old.

Growing up, my dad often would tell me how his father was an absence in his life, but as a kid, I mostly ignored my father's advice until one day in middle school.

I was in eighth grade when I came home crying after being bullied. For some reason, I believed I had to remain friends with this group of guys who were emotionally and verbally abusive to me. I was convinced I couldn't make other friends, so I hated middle school. My dad found me crying in our family room while doing homework on the coffee table. He sat down on the floor across from me and said, "Tell me what happened."

I didn't hold back, and he listened to my rambling explanations.

Then he said, "Brian, you have other friends, right? So what if you just walk away from the bullies and hang out with them? What's the worst that will happen?"

The next day, I dared to sit at a new table for lunch and it made all the difference.

Thirty years later, I mentioned this interaction to my dad when we sat down so I could interview him for this book. The peaty fragrance of scotch filled the room.

"I remember that conversation. But I remember thinking how my father would have never spoken to me like I spoke to you. Your grandpa made it clear that I wasn't to ask questions about bullies or friends. He didn't care that I played baseball or basketball. He didn't care about my desire to do sports. He didn't care when I struggled. He cared for my sisters, but in a very patriarchal sexist way. That was just him and I didn't want to be him for you or your sister."

The comment hung in the air as I geared up to ask the next set of questions. These were going to be harder to ask. I felt as awkward as I did when my dad started the puberty talk and I heard him say "penis."

This time, I felt like I was going to be the one to say "penis" and see my dad flinch.

"Thanks for telling me that, Dad. I think it is because of that moment when you let me cry that I knew I could trust you... and why I am writing this book. So, you ready?" I asked.

He took a sip, smiled almost reveling in my discomfort, and answered, "Of course. Are you?"

Over the next hour and a half, he shared more stories about his dad and how he tried his best to raise me. I'd heard some of his stories before, but most were unknown. It's amazing that even after forty years of being in a relationship with someone, there is always something else to cause you to fall in love with them.

My last question came with our scotch glasses empty and fatigue setting in. It was close to midnight.

"How did you learn to be a good dad if all you had were negative examples?"

He answered, "I learned a lot of it from my mom and reading books. The rest I learned from watching you and your friends and talking with their dads. There wasn't really a manual for who I wanted to be as a dad, so I sort of made some of it up as I went along."

Over the next two weeks, I spoke with friends of my dad. While not my biological dads, I can't underestimate their impact on my formation or my understanding of fatherhood. My sister and I spent countless weekends bouncing between our houses and our friends with parents taking turns watching over our shenanigans.

Each of my "adoptive" dads shared similar responses to my dad about fatherhood and why they were so active in our lives. They wanted to be more involved fathers than the previous generation.

As my best friend's dad put it, "We didn't get you involved in baseball because we thought you were going to the majors. We knew pretty early on that that would never happen. We got you involved because we wanted you to learn about failure and how to connect with your peers. Every time your dad and I took you for ice cream after practice, it was to reflect on practice and to get you to critically think. My father never did that, and your dad and I wanted that for you and Ben."

NEXT STEPS

I was lucky to have a group of dads who cared enough to be present in my young life. Many of the dads who interviewed and have gotten involved with Fathering Together have not. And yet, still, those dads want a deeper connection with their kids. They want their children to know they love them and were there for them whenever times got tough.

In the next chapter, we'll dig into some of their stories and lay the groundwork for how to have a connected dad life.

3

WHO DADS CAN BE

"When I turned four, my birthday wish was to be a dad. I had to wait over thirty years for that wish to come true."

—DANNY M.

No one told me the skills I've been using in the workplace can translate into the home. If they had, I think I would have approached the daunting role of fatherhood a lot more differently. When my daughter was born, I was thirty-three. I'd figured out how to make my way through life as a grown man, then as a husband (sort of), and in only a few months, I had to reframe my life as a dad.

All the hours I'd spent in job trainings, conferences, and graduate classes to make myself more marketable as a professional have home-life applications. I could apply those team building, leadership, and communication skills to my wife and children. Yes, I know my wife and kids are not coworkers or employees, but they are my team. They are my most important team, so why wouldn't I use those skills to improve my life?

The biggest milestone in translating my work-life into a home-life came in the form of a shared electronic calendar. Long gone are the days of forgotten meetings and misplaced post-its. Now, when we have a weekend commitment or the kids have soccer practice, it goes on the calendar and life is good. Or at least, we can now communicate the chaos a little bit better as long as we remember to put it on the calendar!

Once we stumbled upon the calendar strategy, other patterns emerged, and it got me thinking about how much time dads have been conditioned to only think of themselves as their careers. Multiple dads I interviewed shared they had to sacrifice their careers. Some of them grieved the professional they could have been. So entrenched were they in their career ambitions that their child's presence was seen as an obstacle instead of a benefit to them.

While tragic, this shouldn't surprise any of us. In US culture, men put a great amount of effort into their careers. Multiple people have tried breaking down the hours we spend in our lifetimes doing various tasks, and a ballpark number for hours worked is 90,000. This comes behind a staggering 230,000 hours sleeping, but ahead of surfing the internet (28,000 hours) and watching TV (80,000 hours). These numbers were based on a life expectancy of seventy-eight years in 2011.

With so much time spent working, we put more effort into making ourselves worth hiring, not less. We attend professional development conferences, seek certifications and advance degrees, and network within business associations to meet the right person so you get the job you need to support yourself and your family. A lot of us also put off having children because we want to ensure we are stable in our careers. We want to save up money to afford the lifestyle we will want with our children. But what we are actually doing is creating patterns that will be difficult to break.

For dads, this translates into rarely taking time off when our kids finally arrive. In conversations I've had with multiple HR directors at corporations large and small, many offer paid leave policies for dads to take. Some offer as much as six months to a year, but few employees use them. In a study by Boston College in 2011, researchers found two out of three dads said they should be equal partners in caregiving, but less than one in three did so. This could be due to many more male employees (35 percent) than female employees (23 percent) felt care responsibilities hurt their career and more men (40 percent) than women (25 percent) also strongly agreed that "caregivers are perceived to be less committed to their careers than non-caregivers" according to research by the Harvard Business School. In other words, men can appear weak and less committed to the company or work according to the research by Thekla Morgenroth.

During the pandemic, professors Dan Carlson and Richard Petts interviewed over 1,100 married or cohabiting parents with at least one biological child in the home in April 2020 and then again in November 2020. They wanted to see if behavioral changes took place when dads were at home with their kids. They found families had more gender balance in April, but then behaviors reverted to gender-stereotypical chores by November.

Carlson and Petts followed up their research by looking at childcare trends, noticing families without formal childcare resulted in more mothers feeling the strain of employment, but not fathers. Yet, fathers can be care providers; they just don't. Cultural stereotypes are just too entrenched.

But let's for a moment, take a breath and think about a world we want to invent for our children. If the stresses of the pandemic were gone, and we didn't feel trapped in jobs that provide financial and healthcare benefits, there are some amazing opportunities for us.

And this is why my work through Fathering Together is to help men translate their professional identities into personal life strategies and recognize the power of centering your life around your children and not your job is so critical.

As I've said more times than I care to recall, if you can lead a team through a brainstorming meeting to placing a product on the shelf, you have what it takes to get your kids dressed, fed, and to school on time each morning. At the most basic level, it is using project management skills.

REINVENTING MASCULINITY

In 2020, Ed Adams and Ed Frauenheim published *Reinventing Masculinity*. In their preface, they remind us that "the approach to manhood that dominates our culture is unhealthy, outdated, and dangerous." For them, this outdated model of masculinity leads men to be confined to their abilities to express themselves and build meaningful relationships. They filled their book with stories of men going through therapy and realizing how trapped they are by the "Man Box."

Their solution is not to call men toxic, but to work with men to liberate themselves by tapping into their compassion and ability to connect to others. These abilities are not foreign concepts to us, but in recent years, we've let them get rusty. And much like I've shared so far, neither of them admits to being perfect.

When I spoke with Ed Frauenheim for this book, he admitted multiple times to failing in his abilities to connect with his kids and role model healthy behavior. One particular moment took place when his son was only three. Ed couldn't remember the specifics, just that his son looked at him with the stubbornness of a three-nager. Ed's inner child, who had been bullied decades earlier, shouted at Ed to act. So Ed yelled at his son and demanded he go to his room.

Ed acted impulsively when he should have responded developmentally. Seconds later, having calmed himself, Ed realized his behavior shocked him, and the anger he'd unleashed on his toddler. So he went to his son and apologized. Much like my dad, Ed told me he can't recall his father ever apologizing. So Ed took it upon himself to ask his son for forgiveness and show that strength comes in repairing the damage.

In this way, Ed demonstrated a way to untangle the tight links between masculinity, fatherhood, and violence. His son is now well into his teenage years and while they don't always see eye-to-eye, Ed shared that his son's driving lessons haven't been nearly as anger inducing as he expected.

For those unfamiliar with the "Man Box," it is an exercise invented by Paul Kivel and Tony Porter to illustrate the confined masculinity that Adams and Frauenheim explore in their book. When I've done the exercise with college men, they do name positive aspects of masculinity, such as providing and protecting.

But as we unpack those phrases, they are still steeped in patriarchy and power. A father provides, but if they do not relinquish some control in how they provide, children often rebel. If a father protects within empowering their children or equipping them with skills to protect themselves, they will be dependent well into adulthood.

So a new model is needed. A new way to define the masculinity so many fathers hold dear. This new model is taking shape in conversations and workshops by organizations like A Call to Men and Men's Story Project here in the United States, Next Gen Men in Canada, Sonke Gender Justice Center in South Africa, and Equimundo who researches the state of fatherhood across their global network.

In the fall of 2010, I attended a conference on gender-based violence and masculinity. Many of the leaders within the aforementioned organizations attended and throughout the conference, speakers illustrated ways in which they saw men becoming advocates for change. They held deep conversations that deconstructed masculinity and pointed out the negative behaviors we associate with bullies and perpetrators of sexual violence.

The problem I witnessed at that conference, and many more since, is these conversations deconstruct without constructing a new model. As my friend and mentor, Eboo Patel from Interfaith America, once said to me, "It is far easier to criticize than it is to build."

bell hooks wrote in *Feminism is for EVERYBODY* that "what is and was needed is a vision of masculinity where self-esteem and self-love of one's unique being forms the basis of identity." Later in her book, written to and for men, *The Will to Change*, she calls out our reliance on patriarchal structures to maintain our security. She sees men, and fathers, reacting to this fear rather than imagining a better future for themselves and their families.

For my father, he reimagined fatherhood by serving his family. Like many dads, he stepped away from owning his business to take a job as a facilities manager at the local university, where he would work for another twenty-five years.

By doing so, he found additional time to lead fundraising calls for our church. He won a local community award from the United Way as they raised funds for local charities. He attended nearly every baseball game, track meet, and musical performance and chaperoned school trips too.

As a teenager, I never truly appreciated the lengths he and my mom took to sacrifice for us. Even as a dad, I am still discovering the immense well of resources he drew upon to ensure my sister and I got exposed to many opportunities. Watching him with my daughters, helping them do their crafts and learn basic woodworking, it is clear he was always meant to be a dad who happened to work rather than an employee who happened to have kids.

And it makes me wonder how many other men out there pushed aside that identity because society told them to be a man and get a job.

Thankfully, my dad laid a foundation for me and my sister and defined a new way of being a dad. Put another way, he epitomized being a servant leader.

BACKGROUND ON SERVANT LEADERSHIP

Robert Greenleaf coined the phrase "servant leader" in his 1970 essay "The Servant as Leader." He got the idea when reading Hermann Hesse's *Journey to the East*. In the story, the narrator joins a secret society and heads out on an expedition in India. While on this journey, he comes to realize the true leader of his expedition is his servant, Leo. When Leo disappears, everything falls apart. Leo's attention to detail, placing the group ahead of himself, and desire to help others gave him the tenets of a genuine leader.

In "Servant as Leader," Greenleaf saw leadership in crisis. If you didn't know he was writing about the 1960s, you wouldn't be considered foolish. Much of his writing could apply to our current world. Much is in crisis. Between an ongoing pandemic, conspiracy theories running rampant online, and families struggling to manage a crushing burden of information, or lack thereof, to keep their children afloat, optimistic, and empathetic, you could point to anyone as overwhelming.

But this is the stuff of life. I want to say our global crises are heavier than previous generations, but previous generations had their own struggles. Polio, world wars, and the Great Depression defined my grandparents' generation. In the 1800s, the United States had a civil war while also committing genocide against Native American families who still struggle to this day. Meanwhile, European imperialism was carving up Africa, and before that, the Dark Ages ruled over Europe while massive advancements took place in math and science under the Ottoman Empire.

I could go on and on and look further into history, but what is different about today, and our time, is we've never been so interconnected to every other person on Earth. Never have we been able to speak with people around the globe and hear the stories and life experiences in real time. Nor have we seen such strides in equality for women, people of color, and those who identify as LGBTQIA+ while also seeing draconian efforts to undermine those advances.

Threaded through the advances and setbacks is a lack of conversation around fatherhood. So it is time to heed the words of bell hooks and define fatherhood from a place of self-worth and self-love rather than by how much money a dad brings in or how many toys they can provide their children at Christmas or what university their children attend.

Our culture is rapidly changing and using servant leadership as a model for fatherhood is critical for dads to reframe their role and expectations.

ACTIONS OVER WORDS

There's an old saying that tells us actions speak louder than words. Parents learn this pretty quickly when they notice their children mimicking their behavior, and yes, their words too. Children may drop a "shit" or "fuck" in the most embarrassing of situations, but who cares, right? I was driving in bad weather conditions and stopped at a stop sign. I grumbled as we waited for the long line of cars to pass.

From the backseat, I heard, "Dad, are you going to say dammit?"

I glanced in the mirror and asked, "What, Honey?"

My five-year-old replied, "You usually say dammit in these situations."

I forced a smile, then noticed a break in the traffic, and I turned out.

Later, I told my wife, and we had a good laugh. I'll take that humorous anecdote over the constant stream of meltdowns my eldest has when she gets anxious or over-stimulated. In her meltdowns, I see myself when I get stressed. Her lack of resilience may be more acceptable at her age, but the way she melts down, the way she gets angry and lashes out with sarcasm is all me. So it is up to me to change my behavior through role modeling healthy coping mechanisms.

And I've heard similar stories from so many dads. Our actions carry more weight, so what keeps us from changing them? What keeps us from taking on the tenets of servant leadership and leading by better and more holistic examples for our children? Considering fatherhood is malleable, why not create a new form of fatherhood that uses servant leadership as a guide to build stronger emotional bonds and more empowered children?

In Greenleaf's original treatise, he outlines quite a few tenets of servant leadership. One of his followers, Larry C. Spears, narrowed them to ten characteristics in his 2010 article. Ten is still ambitious. And for dads juggling work, home, and who knows what else, I'm going to focus those ten into four main areas: Communication, Other-Oriented, Advocacy, and Community.

COMMUNICATION

If we can't communicate with our children, we are lost. Let's be honest, many of us are lost in the beginning anyway. Our children can only communicate with cries, giggles, and smiles. Many of the dads I've worked with and spoken with for this book have shared they learned quickly the difference between a sleepy cry, a hungry cry, and a dirty diaper cry.

Great fathers take this a step further and learn to pay attention to signals their children pass to them ahead of the "crying" stage. They seek confirmation that we see them, we hear them, and we understand them. Mastering this is critical, but as our children grow and hit developmental milestones, communication lines must be reassessed, and new frameworks built. I'm learning this as my daughter wants to snuggle while watching a movie then a few hours later asserts her independence by making her own dinner and reading to herself before bed.

Jeremy has four daughters, with the oldest preparing for high school graduation and his youngest still in elementary school. Each communicates differently, has different fears, hobbies, and challenges. He's also in a multiracial marriage, so as a white father raising Asian-Pacific Islander children, he has a lot of additional cultural levels to navigate. Yet, through it all, he brings his full self to each relationship and connecting with his daughters on their level.

OTHER-ORIENTED

In Western patriarchal cultures, men are the pinnacle. Laws, social norms, and expectations all have a basis the men are at the center of the story. Thus, to be a connected dad is to be radically counter-cultural because many dads have told me fatherhood means your life is no longer your own. Your life is for your children. My dad closed his company to take a better-paying job. Ross didn't take a job with Microsoft in the early '80s so he could raise his family close to his relatives.

Then there's Matt, who has three children and his youngest, Sam, is gender fluid. Sam was born with male genitalia but prefers wearing dresses. Matt could force a gendered lens on his child's development, but he is choosing to let Sam define himself.

Greenleaf probably didn't have non-binary children in mind when he wrote "The Servant as Leader." But he did write that "the parents who try to raise perfect children are certain to raise neurotics." Matt doesn't want to raise neurotics. Neither do I. And neither do you.

Forcing our children into predetermined pathways and identities will ultimately harm them and undermine the trust we are trying to build within the family. So to be a servant leader dad is to see the world from the eyes of your children and learn everything you can to support them in their development.

ADVOCACY

Greenleaf wrote, "[Foresight] is a better than average guess about what is going to happen when in the future." Being other-oriented will only take us so far. As dads, we must also act. We must advocate for a world we want our children to live in rather than prepare them for the broken world we've inherited. This takes a learner mentality and lots of humility.

One dad friend of mine, Simran Jeet Singh, is Sikh and reports on hate-crimes against Muslims. One day his daughter asked him why no children's book had pictures like them. So he took it upon himself to write one. *Fauja Singh Keeps Going* is a children's book about the oldest marathon runner. When he showed the finished book to his daughter, she smiled and told him how nice it was to see herself reflected on the page.

For Simran, and other dads, they chose to prepare the world for their children instead of preparing their children for the world.

COMMUNITY

Communities have existed longer than human history. Paleontologists have found evidence of dinosaurs living in community. Archaeologists have found hundreds of artifacts showing how hunter-gatherer communities survived harsh conditions. Jared Diamond's book *Guns, Germs, and Steel* incorporates the importance of communities as critical as the domestication of animals for our survival. More recently, Brian Hare and Vanessa Woods surmised that humans' ability to form communities and self-domesticate ourselves created the conditions for us to outmatch Neanderthals and other early humans.

Today, communities look a little different, but they still function on the same level. In 2020, Facebook surveyed hundreds of virtual communities on their platform and found members had similar senses of belonging compared to "real-life" communities.

Most Fathering Together members live nowhere near one another. Yet, they are all connected to a shared identity and purpose: fatherhood. Greenleaf wrote about community as a way for servant leaders to join forces and build stronger healthier communities. For Greenleaf, he saw communities as counter to institutions. Communities are based in love and infused with so much love that members of those communities will "carry into [their] many involvements with institutions which are usually not communities: businesses, churches, governments, schools."

NEXT STEPS

As we proceed through the rest of the book, the four areas will be broken into specific chapters with specific skills that fathers can build to be a strong servant leader for their families. While I name them as skills, you could consider them guidelines, suggestions, and promising practices. Of the hundreds of conversations and fifty-plus formal interviews, no one father had all these practices. Most barely accomplished two or even three. But if we can do our best, strive for the A, and learn something along the way, maybe we'll all be a bit stronger for ourselves, our families, and our communities too.

PART 2

THE PRE-WORK

4

WE'RE NOT PERFECT

"You create a perfect framework in your mind and then every-thing breaks down as soon as the baby gets here."

—JASON H.

Let's get this out of the way from the very beginning: you can't predict the future. You might think you are going to be the perfect parent, but you'd be fooling yourself.

You are not perfect. Neither am I. Neither is anyone else.

In an interview with *Business Insider*, Sara Blakely, Spanx founder, shared how her father asked her every night at dinner what failures she had during the day. While it may sound negative, her father wanted her to make sure she was never settling, that she was always striving and making mistakes.

In those mistakes, we grow. My daughter is naturally gifted in math. Her second-grade teacher has been telling us she recommended getting her a math tutor because she's so far ahead of her classmates. I don't share this to brag. I'm actually scared out of my mind because how am I supposed to teach her if she knows more math than I do?

I share this because she's constantly telling me she gets everything right on her homework and she likes it. When I shared the Sara Blakely story about learning from our mistakes, she didn't get it. She didn't want to be tested. So I asked her, "How will you know how much you know if you never get anything wrong?"

She didn't answer me right away, but a few weeks later, she found an app on her iPad that had math lessons for every grade level. She smiled and said, "Dad, let's see how many of these things I know!"

So I jumped to the calculus tab and pulled up limits. I never understood limits in high school, and I was pretty confident she wouldn't know them either. She took one look at the screen and laughed. "I'm not ready for that."

If you've been through a professional growth or mentorship program, you've probably encountered the comfort zone diagram. Most diagrams present three concentric circles. The inner circle is the comfort zone, followed by discomfort, and finally panic or paralysis. Studies have shown we learn best in our discomfort zone. When lessons offer the right amount of discomfort, we grow. If we step too far, we shut down because it is too hard or beyond our comprehension, like my daughter seeing the limit equation.

We can't always live in discomfort, but we definitely can't live in the comfort zone forever, either.

I've met people who love the comfort zone and stand confidently within it and project an image of perfection. If you're a dad and you're doing this, two problems can arise:

your child will either see you as perfect and strive to be perfect and end up failing without the means to recover, or they will see right through you and lose trust in your ability to be authentic with them.

In both situations, kids will learn the wrong lesson.

We don't want them striving for perfection because perfectionism carries with it a host of mental health problems. Dr. Paul Hewitt, a clinical psychologist, focuses his research on perfectionism. From his research, he sees perfectionism as connected to psychological, relational, physical, and achievement dysfunction. By seeking perfection, we are actually placing barriers to deep connection and happiness because we are unwilling to allow people to see our faults, our humanity.

So don't pressure yourself to be perfect for your kids and definitely don't pressure them to be perfect either.

Executive coach and friend, Mike Zeller, told me one day, "Progress over obsession is perfection!" When we strive to make daily progress at work or at home, we will have moments of failure, but we make progress and learn. When we obsess over perfection, we get stuck.

Don't get stuck.

Don't let your kids get stuck either.

Just be real and authentic with your gifts, talents (and faults too). Your relationship will be stronger for it.

5

DOING THE DEEP WORK

"Do it for her."

—HOMER SIMPSON

In a classic *The Simpsons* episode, Homer quits his job at the power plant only to return, groveling when he finds out his third child, Maggie, is on the way. Mr. Burns agrees but offers Homer a "demotivational plaque" that reads: "Don't forget: you're here forever." But in the concluding shot of the episode, the camera pans over the plaque, and we see that Homer has placed photos of Maggie over the words so that it only reads: "Do it for her."

You don't have to have seen this episode to have seen the image of that plaque. Go to any dad group on the internet and chances are you'll see a meme or a post with it. Many of the dads in my dad group often use it when posting about what they have to endure in their day-to-day in order to support their families.

I have many memories from our family dinner table where my dad complained about work and what he endured, and what he gave up to support his family. When I was very young, he co-owned a woodworking business. Every time I get a whiff of turpentine or shellack, I'm teleported to his warehouse, where lumber and antique furniture filled the air with the pungent aroma. Yet, like many small businesses, it didn't last. He had a falling out with his partner and the income wasn't enough to support his growing family. So, he took a job at Purdue University in the facility services department.

Despite many hard days, he had a lot of great days, too. And like most kids, I didn't see my dad as an entry-point employee. I thought it was incredible he had keys to get into almost any building on campus and that he had special parking privileges at major events. He was my dad! He was my hero. And thankfully, where Homer failed time and time again in the fatherhood department, my father soared.

While I don't mean to compare my father with a cartoon character, I do want to point out my dad prepared for fatherhood. He was emotionally supportive and wasn't an inept buffoon like Homer Simpson. The humor that stems from this buffoonery left me in stitches as a kid, but as I watch episodes now, I don't understand how Marge stood by him after so many countless faults. Nor do I appreciate how millions of kids grew up with Homer Simpson as a default father figure. But anyone in my generation would easily list him along with Danny Tanner from *Full House*, Bill Cosby (because we didn't know what we know now) and Dr. Jason Seaver from *Growing Pains* as some of the most well-known dads of the late 1980s with Carl Winslow from *Family Matters*, and Uncle Phil from *Fresh Prince of Bel-Air* and Tim the Toolman Taylor from *Home Improvement* joining the list in the early 1990s.

Homer Simpson stands apart for his complete ineptitude. Sure he saves the city from a nuclear meltdown, but he did it by playing "Eeny-Meeny-Miny-Moe" and his ineptitude affects others too (check out the "Oh Brother, Where Art Thou?" episode). The other dads make mistakes, as any father will, but all step up and show emotional depth and care. Nearly every father knows the Uncle Phil scene in "Papa's Got a Brand New Excuse" or the numerous scenes of Danny Tanner listening to his daughter's feelings and making them feel important.

What is tragic about Homer Simpson is his inability to make meaning and reflect on his impact on his kids. In this way, he presents a caricature of fatherhood, but one not far from the mark. Many dads I spoke with for this book and who join our Facebook community often talk about what they do for their children and how they support their children, but few talk about who they are for their children.

I can't overstate this enough that becoming a fatherhood is the biggest job you'll ever take on, and yet, unlike the preparation many of us do to get that next dream job, we don't prepare a resume. One dad even admitted to reading nothing because he didn't want to be influenced by others and that he would leave the direction of his child's upbringing to his wife.

While Homer is designed to elicit laughter and some contempt, there is nothing funny about not preparing internally for the biggest job in the world. Homer provides an important lesson behind the humor.

TAKING TIME FOR PHYSICAL AND MENTAL PREPARATION

Ted Gonder is an extremely proud and outspoken dad of three boys. In the past few years, he's taken to coaching other expecting dads on getting physically fit as they prepare to welcome their children into the world. He does this because he sees a lack of intention in the world for fathers and their role in the family. Needless to say, we hit it off immediately.

When I asked Ted when he knew he was going to be a dad, I didn't realize his wife was sitting beside him. We were talking over the phone, no Zoom screens or virtual connection, just two guys connecting old school.

Technically, his wife answered my question first, with a guffaw and a quick, muffled sorry. Then Ted replied, "I knew I wanted to be a dad after my wife and I decided to keep our son."

"Everything okay over there?" I asked.

I heard some shuffling around and giggles, then Ted replied. "No, my wife is just reminding me of how we came to the decision together."

In the background I heard Franzi clear her throat in agreement. Having never spoken to Franzi one-on-one at that point, I was nervous knowing she would overhear the conversation, but knowing their relationship, I knew whatever I would ask Ted wouldn't be something the two of them hadn't discussed. And as Ted and I continued our conversation, that became abundantly clear.

Ted continued explaining how he and his wife, Franzi, had been dating long-distance. He was in Chicago; she was in Berlin. Due to the distance, they got serious quickly because flights weren't cheap and one of them was going to have to make a major decision on relocation. So on one late night conversation, Franzi asked Ted, "Do you think you'll want to have kids within a year?"

Ted responded with, "How about within seven years?"

She countered with, "How about two?"

Ultimately, they settled on a window of two to four years, and she moved to Chicago. As luck would have it, in their celebration of her move, they got pregnant much sooner than two to four years.

The night before they took the pregnancy test to confirm Franzi's suspicions, Ted had a breakdown. It stemmed from his fear of being an inadequate father. Ted was an only child, and while his family was very supportive, they were emotionally distant and raising children had never entered their conversations. Plus, outside of school, he hadn't really been exposed to other children, and he'd never really processed what becoming a dad would mean.

Similar to Homer Simpson, the new reality scared him, and he couldn't cope. Unlike Homer Simpson, he didn't quit his job or slack off in his preparation. Instead, he and Franzi took time to evaluate themselves, their relationship, and if they were ready to have this child. They rented a car and drove to a Zen garden where they meditated and made a decision tree with pros and cons. Ted emphasized the list was based on the emotional impact this child would have on them, but logistical stuff crept in too, like childcare and family support.

Ted concluded, "The pros of moving forward and having this baby and keeping this baby and investing in this baby so far outweighed any con we could come up with."

Upon returning to their daily lives, Ted understood the foundation for him to be a good father was shared between his own mental health and the relationship he had with Franzi. For Ted, if their relationship wasn't solid, if they had doubts, it would only serve to negatively impact their child.

In order to ensure the relationship was successful, Ted had to work on his physical and mental health first. He had been pushing long hours to get his non-profit start-up off the ground. With the imbalance of sleep and personal versus professional obligations, he'd leaned heavily on alcohol and coffee to get him through the day. Thus, his gut was expanding, and his mental health was flailing.

So he pushed himself to turn it around. He began exercising every day and reducing his consumption of alcohol and coffee to bring better balance into his life and integrating the values he was building for his family into his professional career.

Now, with his wife and three sons, Ted lives a much more balanced life and has stepped away from his non-profit to a less demanding job that allows him time to coach other dads as they begin their fatherhood journey.

A CASE FOR EMOTIONAL PREPARATION

Another dad I connected with, Phil, shared a very different story. He and his wife struggled to get pregnant. For a year, they tried the natural way, but when this failed, they began connecting with a fertility specialist. This led to months of medications, tests, supplements, and more money than he cares to remember. In the end, they went through in vitro fertilization, or IVF.

Complicating matters for them was insurance, or more specifically, the insurance benefit for IVF that was going to end within two months. So they rushed into IVF and while he wanted to enjoy the journey, he found himself focused on logistics and money management, not reading *What to Expect When You're Expecting* or diving into the deep work like Ted. "There just wasn't time," Phil remembered thinking.

Throughout the entire process, nothing seemed to go as planned for them. The doctors weren't able to harvest as many eggs as they hoped and then only one embryo survived long enough to be transferred but ended in a miscarriage a few weeks later.

"It almost broke us," Phil shared with me, "but the desire to be parents was as strong as ever."

Then miraculously, they got pregnant without any interventions. Phil found himself ready to rejoice and prepare the home for their newborn. But once again, their joy was trampled by the onset of the COVID-19 pandemic. Being stuck at home, their celebrations were muted.

This muted joy carried through the pregnancy into the first year of their son's life. Phil found himself increasingly isolated and disconnected from other dads. The emotional, physical, and financial stress of infertility, a miracle pregnancy during a pandemic, and a lack of close male friendships created a fatherhood journey he didn't recognize.

It was a fatherhood journey many share, including myself, and it's why I created Fathering Together in the first place. Fathers don't have to be alone. We don't have to be isolated, but too many of us don't stop to realize this.

Phil's journey through IVF is not uncommon either, and many dads with whom I spoke for this book shared similar experiences. When the miscarriages took place, their wives received outpourings of support, but they received relatively little. This lack of community and support has a self-fulfilling prophecy effect on these dads.

First, in general, our society doesn't teach men to be emotionally expressive. So when tough situations happen, we bottle it up.

Second, society doesn't socialize us to create communities of support. So when a crisis occurs, we turn inward.

When these two conditions take place, where does a man who wants to be a dad turn to when disaster strikes? If they see their partners receiving support and they are left alone, this confirms the stereotypes.

So, what we need is a space for dads to be expressive and supported, and within that space, dads need to prepare for fatherhood. As mentioned in chapter two, so many of my peers expect to be dads, but they don't have plans. They don't prepare and scramble for support late in the game.

When dads are scrambling and left without a secure place or role to play, they can feel even more disconnected and isolated, like Phil. But when they take the time to do some deep work, they can build an emotional foundation for themselves and their families, like Ted.

THE FATHERHOOD CORE 5
At Fathering Together, we've developed the Fatherhood Core 5 to address this foundation. The five elements focus on cognitive, financial, physical, social-emotional, and spiritual health. They are loosely derived from Maslow's hierarchy of needs theory.

In his theory, Maslow created a universal set of needs we must fulfill in order to grow and develop in our lives. It begins with physiological needs, like food and shelter, then moves to safety needs like personal and financial security. The upper levels focus on relationships and self-worth that must be fulfilled before attaining self-actualization.

The only problem with his theory is most of us don't go through these stages linearly. While it makes sense that having stable food sources and financial security comes before feelings of self-worth and caring for others, Maslow only focused on college students who came from wealthy families.

Therefore, at Fathering Together, we don't focus on the hierarchy as much as the areas of health that build a foundation for strong relationships with our children, families, and community. In order to create this foundation, our workshops and discussions are all based in at least one area of the aforementioned areas. Through group dialogue and workshops, dads can connect and gain insights into better practices as they prepare to become dads or reconnect with their kids as they navigate their development.

Take Ted and Phil. Both found out they were going to be dads. Ted took the time to address his mental health and lay a foundation for growth in himself, his relationship with his wife, and ultimately his kids. Phil wasn't able to do this and has struggled to build connections because he hadn't done the internal work.

Thankfully, both have benefited from joining groups like Fathering Together. Ted can provide insights and strategies to new dads, like Phil. Phil can find support and accountability for his additional responsibilities.

POST-PARTUM DEPRESSION ISN'T JUST FOR MOMS

Fathering Together is not the only organization out there. Kevin Gruenberg co-founded Love, Dad in 2016 with Richard Cohen to address the absence of father engagement in policies and practices in home visitation. Since then, their work has focused on perinatal health in dads.

As I shared in chapter one, I felt increasingly isolated after my first daughter was born. I turned inward instead of seeking help. This is not uncommon. As Kevin will tell you, on average 25 percent of dads experience postpartum depression and if their partner is experiencing it, the probability for the father jumps to nearly 50 percent.

A year ago, Kevin and I sat on a panel with two other dads. When we shared the story of becoming a father, all of us said something like, "Well, I definitely struggled, but I wouldn't say I was depressed." Kevin went last on the panel and reminded us all of the aforementioned statistics and since four of us sat on the panel, most likely, one of us had experienced post-partum depression.

As Kevin will tell you, depression expresses itself differently in different people. And depending on its severity, someone could feel mildly depressed and need a support group to work through their feelings, or their experience could be severe needing medication and long-term care. In 2019 alone, the National Institute of Mental Health estimated that 19.4 million adults, or 7.8 percent of all adults in the United States had at least one episode of major depression.

Since the onset of the pandemic, these numbers have increased with more and more attention being called to address mental health, burnout, and anxiety. So, for the sake of our children, we need to take our mental health seriously and make sure we are doing the deep work associated with it.

Increasingly, I've become more vocal in my conversations with dads about my mental health too. I'm honest about the medications I take to help me control my anxiety and mood. By doing so, we destigmatize mental health and the challenges that come with it. As I mentioned in the introduction, my daughter called me out on poor decisions and negative behavior toward her. While it hurt, she wasn't wrong.

And I tried changing my behavior and tried new approaches for managing my stress and my angry outbursts. However, running a business isn't easy. Running a family isn't easy either. When you add the stresses of a pandemic, the recipe can end in disaster. So I sought therapy, spiritual direction, and finally medication.

I'll be honest, my ego took a hit. I didn't want to be that guy who relied on medications. I thought I could control it, but for every one of my outbursts at my children's misbehavior, it was magnified back at me. I set the wrong example for my daughters and our household was the worst for it.

As I talk with more dads about my mental health and weave it into conversations and coaching calls, the more I find other dads are in the same boat. It's like a barrier comes down and the elephant in the room, that we didn't notice or recognize, is now in plain sight. The hesitant responses to how we manage the stresses in life are more open and authentic.

When I spoke with one dad in particular during the interviews for this book, his reaction to my use of medication took me by surprise.

"Join the club!" He laughed over the phone. "I've been on meds since I was a kid and when I took a vacation from them in college, it wasn't pretty."

"Really? I never would have guessed," I reacted.

"Oh yeah, being on anti-anxiety medications makes me a better father because I can focus on what matters."

And as Homer Simpson, despite all his failings, reminds us, all the deep work and hard truths we must face serve the benefit of our children. As we will learn in the chapters ahead, the deep work lays the groundwork for being a servant leader to our children.

NEXT STEPS

In the next section, we'll be diving into the first characteristic of servant leadership: Communication. As we all know, communication comes in many forms, from verbal and non-verbal, to the depth of attention we give it. Our children naturally understand this and it's something I've had to relearn with them along the way.

PART 3

COMMUNICATION

6

BEING PRESENT

"The best advice I got from another parent is you won't know what to do sometimes and usually in the middle of the night, you just have to hold your baby while they are crying and all you can do is hold them and love them."

—ANDY K.

"Dad, look at me when I'm talking to you. Don't you respect me?" my eight-year-old shouts as I grab cold medicine.

"Where did you learn to say that?" I ask. I put down the cold medicine and turn my full attention to her.

"I don't know. Everywhere." She purses her lips and continues, "I said, my stomach hurts. I need a probiotic before you pack them."

We were packing for my two daughters to go to their grandparents' for the week. We were working our way down the list from medicine to toiletries to clothing, and I'll admit, I wasn't fully present in every aspect of the conversation.

This wasn't the first time, either. I would wager to guess many of us hold conversations with our children while multi-tasking. Whether it is making dinner, answering emails on our phones, or any number of mundane tasks required of our day, we all fall prey to the busyness of life.

Most children aren't aware of just how busy parents are. They want to talk to us, and they want our full attention. Period.

For most of us, we only get eighteen years to have them in our care. In the beginning, that time feels like forever, but most parents will admit time doesn't feel linear. It feels exponential and as they get older, quality moments of connection seem to shrink.

So how do we ensure to make the most of those opportunities? Former FBI agent, Dr. Jack Schafer, has an answer.

THE FRIENDSHIP FORMULA

In 2015, Dr. Jack Schafer published *The Like Switch*. In the book, he presents four criteria for becoming friends with someone that he calls the Friendship Formula. These criteria are proximity, frequency, duration, and intensity. His goal was to help people navigate social situations. His goal wasn't to look at the relationship between dad and child.

Yet, as I read his book, the application made total sense, and my maternal grandfather kept coming up for me. My grandpa lived his life with these four criteria embedded in his thoughts and actions. He and my grandmother had sixty-four amazing years of marriage that included seven children, sixteen grandchildren, and a growing list of great-grandchildren. I have countless memories of spending time at their house and them babysitting us while my parents took vacations.

On his eightieth birthday, my aunts and uncles gathered to celebrate his life and tried to capture some of his stories because my grandmother had just passed. We weren't sure how many more years we'd get with him.

During the visit, they took turns reading letters my grandfather wrote to my grandmother while he was deployed to Europe during World War II. In one letter, he lamented about his second son, Wayne. "I'll be here longer than I initially thought so I guess I won't know what Wayne will be as a little boy."

My grandfather died ten years ago, so I can't verify this belief, but this one sentence confirms my grandfather lived by the Friendship Formula. He applied this formula everywhere. He lived his entire life in South Bend, Indiana, until my parents moved him into a retirement community, but even then, he was a regular at euchre night.

His dedication to his community meant he share space with his family, friends, and neighbors to learn their stories and understand what they needed in their relationship to him. This made him a well-respected businessman with several local businesses to his credit. He became a leader in his church and the Knights of Columbus, and as a veteran, he made attending his local VFW a regular occurrence. It wasn't just that he shared space or met frequently, but he made sure the depth of his engagement had meaning. When I joined him for a Knights of Columbus spaghetti dinner, he had a story for everyone we met, and they had one for my grandfather.

My grandfather was never rich, though he sent all his children to college. He wasn't famous either, but he had a rich life by giving himself to the friendships around him and ensuring his children had a stable family for when life got rough.

To be clear, there is a fine line between being friends with your child and parenting them. My grandfather, for all his love and affection, could still be as stern as anyone. I remember ignoring my chores to go play with my neighborhood friends. It was a gorgeous sunny weekend, and our backyard ravine begged for me and my friends to have an adventure. We were building a dam in the little creek when I heard him calling my name. When I stepped from the shade of a tree into my backyard, I saw his scowl. His crossed arms over his chest told me I had let him down.

He didn't yell. He played the disappointment card, and I felt terrible. I called down to my friends to finish the dam without me and the rest of the day, I cleaned the house and felt the weight of shame on my shoulders.

Later, when my parents returned from their trip, I confessed to my mom, who told me I got off easy. "He's going soft in his old age," she laughed before reminding me to listen better the next time.

In the last few years of his life, anytime I returned to my hometown, I scheduled time with him at his retirement community. His body was shutting down, but his mind was as quick as ever. He'd share stories from his youth, reflect on my adventures and lack of chores with me, and remind me he would love to see me get married before he joined grandma in heaven.

When I told him I met someone special, he demanded I visit and introduce me to her. A year later, when I told him I proposed, he smiled and said, "About time!"

He would die in his sleep two weeks later.

SOMETIMES PRESENCE IS ALL YOU'VE GOT

Andy is a dad who follows in the same mold as my grandpa. He's a natural educator and has worked in non-profit organizations most of his life. I met him when our professional lives crossed paths for a year at the same company.

Much of Andy's commitment to his work and his family is based in his Jewish faith. He's raising his two kids, who are under the age of ten, to be committed to community and repairing the world, which is based on a passage from the Book of Isaiah. In this way, he's teaching them to spot where the community most needs their gifts and talents and to live a life of servant leadership. When I posted about my fatherhood project and asked for interviews, he jumped at the chance to share his story.

When I asked him about his own father, he spoke about the need to perform and earn his father's love. His father worked long hours, so family dinner was the only regular time for Andy's chance at interaction. Yet, the interactions were often one-sided. Andy would talk his father's ear off about his day, trying to earn his father's respect and attention. But, most of the time, his father would just nod along, distracted by other responsibilities and tasks.

The most attention Andy got came during baseball games or school theater productions. His father would praise him for his performance, so Andy tried getting better at sports. He put more time into acting. Andy is a masterful storyteller, but he was not destined for major league sports. So his efforts to win his father's attention became less frequent and their interactions less intimate. Today, he rarely speaks with him.

So when his first child came along, Andy was there from the start. He made sure to get home and play with his newborn as much as possible and not send any signs that his child had to perform to win his love. He was gushing with it.

Shortly after his wife returned to work, she had to go on a business trip. Andy was ready. He'd prepped meals, formula, and activities. Then, his son started sneezing and crying after daycare. Being only nine months old, his son couldn't tell Andy what was wrong, so Andy did everything the books said to do. He took his temperature. It was high, but not dangerously high. He rocked him, but his son didn't want to be held. He tried distracting him with toys, but nothing could console his son.

As day shifted to night, Andy's son was exhausted from the bug he'd caught. Andy gave him medicine, which calmed him, but he wouldn't lie down. Being horizontal on his back only made breathing worse. So Andy found himself sitting in the rocking chair beside the crib, holding his nine-month-old throughout the night.

For hours Andy rocked back and forth, humming random songs, and staring at his baby who wheezed and sneezed the night away. There was nothing more Andy knew to do but be present and hold his child.

Eight years later, Andy got choked up relaying the story to me. "I felt like a failure until the next day when my friend reminded me that sometimes all we can do is be present."

Ever since, Andy has been present. He helps at his kid's school and goes on field trips. He builds Lego structures and invites his children to help with dinner. He lives and breathes the Friendship Formula to ensure they know he is someone they can trust.

IT'S THE SMALL THINGS THAT ARE IMPORTANT

If you've attended a business seminar on time management, you've probably heard the life lesson that focuses on putting the big rocks into the jar before the sand. My friend and colleague, Brandon Smith, applies this concept to fatherhood. He and Andy have never met, but they are definitely cut from the same cloth.

Brandon is better known as the "workplace therapist." He's a regular contributor to major news outlets, speaks at conferences, and consults with organizations to help them improve workplace culture, retention, and more. His smile is disarming, and his enthusiasm is contagious, even through a computer screen on a Zoom call.

He joined me for a work-life integration conversation where he shared his fatherhood journey with the group.

"Early on, when my first child was still in diapers, I needed a new job, and got approached by a major Fortune 500 company. It was the opportunity of a lifetime, but the job required frequent travel and long hours. I knew if I took the job, we'd be set financially, but it would come at the cost of my relationship to my children. So I turned it down.

"My dad was never around for me. He showed up for my graduation. He showed up when I got an award, but my mom and grandma raised me. They were there for all the small things, the daily check-ins, parent-teacher meetings, etc. I wanted to be there for my children. So I figured out another way to earn a living that enables me to show up for every little league game and family dinners.

"And this is what I'll leave with you all today. I made sure that each child got one big trip with me. When they turn thirteen, I take all of them on a trip to somewhere in the United States. It's just the two of us and my youngest has been dying to go to Disney World for his trip. So if you have the means to do it, make sure you're there for all the small things and fit in a big one too!"

I mentioned having read *The Like Switch*, and he smiled back at me. "I've read it too, and it makes for a great template for the relationship I have with my kids. I don't need to be their best friend, but I do need them to know that I'm there for them when they need me."

NEXT STEPS
Much like my grandpa, Andy and Brandon are forging bonds with their kids that will last well into adulthood. Both aren't afraid to have disciplinary talks with their kids, but that discipline is enclosed within a structure of frequent attention, long periods of play, and deep connection.

It is within the deep connections that makes for the most impact. In the next chapter, we'll dive emotional expression and the importance of building empathy with our children. For Greenleaf, this was critical in the workplace, where he saw good supervisors taking time to connect with their staff and identify their staff's strengths to help them grow and develop as leaders.

For those with strong dad-first mindsets, the same is true for our children. I nearly lost the chance with my daughters a year ago when I was overworking myself. But when my daughter called me out, it was a clarion call for me. I'll continue to make mistakes and miss opportunities like when I travel for work. But I make sure I'm there to tuck them in as often as possible, because we only get eighteen years until they become adults.

7

BEING EMOTIONALLY COURAGEOUS

"I just lost my shit. I yelled and left the room."

—ED F.

Servant leadership begins with empathy, and you can't have empathy without understanding emotions and expressing those emotions. I have no clue how many words are in the English language that pertain to emotions. On some level, that is a matter of interpretation, I guess.

But I know there are more than three.

I say three because many of my colleagues, who hold trainings on emotional intelligence, talk about how men are allowed to be mad, sad, and glad. These three define the range of socially acceptable expressions. We can laugh, we can get violently angry, and sometimes we can cry. The tears are generally allowed at the death of a loved one or sports, but even then it is debatable.

If three emotions are all that our culture allows men, then our culture fails all of us. As dads, we are operating at a deficit, and it is up to us to solve it. Because how are we supposed to educate our children to be emotionally expressive if we can't be emotionally expressive ourselves?

If we can't explain the difference between joy and happiness or frustration and anger, our children won't either, or they will turn to someone else for help.

One truly heartbreaking story comes out of Romania under the brutal regime of Nicolae Ceaușescu. He outlawed abortion and contraception because he believed an increase in the population would spur economic growth. His policy led to hundreds of children being orphaned. By the 1980s, the strain on the orphanage system meant staff were underprepared to support so many children. Thus, babies and young children would cry for hours with no one attending to their emotional needs. They had to learn to comfort themselves, which meant they learned no one was there to help them. So why bother crying?

As those children grew, they struggled to build attachments with other individuals. They couldn't attach so they couldn't empathize or understand what others were experiencing.

While this is an extreme example, it highlights how critical it is that we, as dads, educate ourselves to have the emotional language and awareness for our children. We must be able to express ourselves, to express our sorrow, our grief, our humor, our joy, our frustration, and our longing. By doing so, our children can learn to trust us with their emotions and come to us with the challenges they face.

THE LONG ROAD TO EQUITY

In the fall of 2021, I gave a workshop on establishing gender equity at home for the National At-Home Dad Network. Halfway through my presentation, a participant raised his hand.

"I hulk out when communication breaks down," the dad said. Around the room, I saw several other dads nodding in agreement. The comment didn't surprise me.

I had asked the group, "What happens when you face challenges at home when you try to implement new strategies for managing chores?" This participant's raw honesty and the reaction from others took our conversation in a whole new direction.

So, we focused on anger management and how to respond rather than react. For most in the room, the realization of the difference was earth shattering. One participant shared that he often fell into a "fixer" mentality where he tried to solve the issue as quickly as possible. Sometimes he'd attempt to make the situation a teaching moment, but most of the time, he'd just react.

Afterward, several came up to me and said they weren't expecting a class on anger management, but they appreciated the space to open up and share their feelings.

One dad, who was doing a workshop on mental health later in the day, came up and said, "See why I run my mental health workshop twice at this conference? Dads need it more than we realize!"

I smiled and added, "But isn't it interesting how our culture tells us that men should only express being glad, mad, or sad?"

I know lots of people who lead workshops on emotional intelligence, and they've begun incorporating issues of DEI (diversity, equity, and inclusion) too. While they all have slight variations to their styles and messages, the core to almost every workshop I've attended comes down to relationships. To be more emotionally intelligent, to lead with a DEI-mindset, you must have an eye toward building relationships with others.

This came through during my workshop with the at-home dads. When I asked how many set up the playdates for their kids, a handful of hands went up. When I followed up asking why their kid was best friends with those kids on the playdates, fewer hands went up. It is just as critical for our children to see that we care and invest emotionally in them as it is setting up space for them to play with their friends.

The same is true in the workplace. To get teams to perform effectively and efficiently, supervisors and managers must learn how their team thinks and what motivates them to perform. Our children are the same way. If your child is having a meltdown, yelling at them to start won't solve anything, but distracting them with their favorite toy might.

For dads to build those relationships and show our investment, we must be able to express more emotional complexity than glad, mad, and sad.

HECTOR AND THE SEARCH FOR HAPPINESS

I'm a huge fan of the actor Simon Pegg. In 2014, he starred in a film called *Hector and the Search for Happiness*. It's based on a book by the same name. The story follows a psychologist who is stuck in his life. He struggles to connect with his patients. He and his girlfriend aren't on the same page in their relationship either. So he travels around the world to wake himself up and uncover the truth about happiness.

In the end, he undergoes a brain scan when reacting to questions from a researcher played by Christopher Plummer. He's supposed to conjure images that are meaningful to him. When he does this, the digital image of his brain will light up based on the chemical reactions. For Hector, the images he conjures are not "those of a grown man." The researcher and his ex-girlfriend encourage him to dig deeper, but then his current girlfriend calls. While on the phone, he has an emotional breakthrough and connects with her on a deeper level like never before. Then his brain scan lights up and his former girlfriend and the researcher cheer him on.

While the movie got mixed reviews, I loved its message. And that is highlighting the importance of digging deeper into our emotional connections rather than our daily transactions. The final scenes of the movie portray Hector doing exactly what he did in the beginning. He returned to his girlfriend and his psychiatry practice, but this time, he's connecting and understanding with his clients like never before.

As dads, we need to do this too. If we only believe ourselves to be financial and structural supports to our families, we will miss out on the emotional joys and challenges.

So how do we get there? How do we not hulk out and react poorly and instead respond through empathy and connection?

THREE STEPS TO BUILDING EMPATHY

THE BRAIN SCIENCE
First, you have to understand the brain science. When our brains receive information, the cerebellum gets the signal first. The cerebellum is near the bottom of the brain, beside the brain stem, and it handles much of our muscles' movements and our instinctual reactions. These are the fight, flight, and freeze reactions.

Any signal, whether it is a screaming boss, a charging bear, or a child looking for a hug, travels through the cerebellum before going into the cerebrum, which processes higher functions before going to the rest of our brain. The reason for this is if we are faced with a bear charging us in the wilderness, we don't want to be stuck contemplating an existential crisis or analyzing its gait. We want to get away and to safety as quickly as possible. So our instincts kick in and we react.

But our children are not bears even when they may act like it. So we need to respond to them from our frontal lobe that processes higher functions.

RESPOND, DON'T REACT

The Institute for Health and Human Potential does a lot of work with people to coach them on how to bypass the cerebellum reactions in the workplace. When I took a training with them four years ago, all I could think about was how effective this would be with my kids. By recognizing how my body could react when faced with a challenge from my children, I could take a deep breath and respond rather than react.

But the response must be developmentally appropriate or else the metaphorical head butting will continue.

So we need to ensure we are building empathy with our children and, just as importantly, we need to build empathy in ourselves.

Researcher and author Jamil Zaki's book, *The War for Kindness*, takes an expansive look into empathy. From the history of studying it to modern applications and developing empathy in children, the book covers a lot of ground. But his use of Gene Roddenberry's *Star Trek* sold me on his approach.

The "Roddenberry hypothesis" is that empathy is both a trait (something fixed that we either have or don't have) and it is a reflex. While research on twins shows that empathy varies between individuals, there is plenty of additional research that highlights empathy can be built up and strengthen, like a muscle.

What I found most fascinating from the research Zaki pulled together is those who inflict bad news and stress upon others develop less empathy. Zaki points to oncologists who struggle to deliver heartbreaking news to loved ones when cancer wins. However, the opposite is true: those who endure pain and heartache increase their empathy. For example, victims of hurricanes are more likely to support others who are victimized by the same natural disasters.

As I spoke with dads for this book, I found many dads who struggled with being taskmasters and punishing their children when they made bad choices. While not the same as delivering cancer diagnoses, there is still a level of emotional distance dads go through when placing their children in timeout.

The dads in my gender equity workshop played into this as well. After the dad confessed to "hulking out," another shared how he would often berate his staff in ways he never would his children. He had been an executive chef before becoming the at-home parent. He'd lay into his dishwashers for arriving late and chastise line cooks for not following instructions.

He was not showing empathy to others. In his mind, their relationship was transactional. They were there to serve a purpose, not to be a family. And to some extent, this makes sense. A restaurant wouldn't last very long if every meal you ordered was fraught with family drama and discussion rather than execution and defined roles.

But the us-versus-them thinking and transactional mindsets keep us from truly connecting. Elsewhere in his book, Zaki highlights how men tend to show less empathy than women. The difference between their empathy scores is minimized when you introduce an incentive. For men, the incentive was sex and money.

So what incentives will drive dads to be more empathic and build empathy in their children? It is easier said (or written in this case) than done, but the following chapters will go into more detail, but what they all have in common is our second step: social-emotional learning.

Ensuring your children have social-emotional learning (SEL) in their school system or exposure at home is critical. SEL focuses on how we feel and regulate our emotions. In the introduction to this book, I mentioned how my five-year-old asked how my day was going and told me to do some self-talk to help me improve. This is classic SEL. Talking to yourself, identifying your own emotions, and processing those emotions are the foundation.

The problem is men rarely take opportunities to know their emotions. Being glad, mad, and sad doesn't give you a rich vocabulary upon which to build, but we can break that cycle and provide that language to our children while learning it ourselves.

TAKE A RISK AND BE VULNERABLE

This brings us to the third and final step: take a risk and be vulnerable.

At Fathering Together, we do this through our DadChats. These monthly meetups allow for dads to connect and share stories. While Zoom calls aren't the most intimate spaces, they do offer a chance for connection and a relationship to build.

During one of the DadChats, we discussed birth stories. We went around the Zoom "room" and shared what it was like to be present for the birth of our children. A common theme emerged.

Joe went first and shared how he never imagined standing in the hallway while doctors took his wife to the operation room for an emergency C-Section. It wasn't in their birth plan.

Then, Stan went next and shared a similar story and added, "While I was getting the scrubs on, a nurse came out of the operating room and said, 'If something should go wrong, we need to know who to save... your wife or child.'"

A few dads later, Bryan mentioned he and his wife had gone through two miscarriages and even while he stood beside his wife and saw his son's head beginning to emerge, he still didn't get his hopes up. Then, when he held his crying newborn in his arms, he allowed himself hope and joy. As he told all of us, "I didn't realize how much I had been holding my emotions at bay to be strong for my wife because the miscarriages nearly tore us apart."

I took those experiences and asked other dads, for this book, what their preparation for fatherhood looked like. Many shared they had read books. Some attended courses with their wife at the hospital to learn about coaching techniques, how to put on diapers and such. But across the board, none of us remember any part of the process where we covered what we all shared during the DadChat.

For all the advances in modern science, giving birth to a child still has major risks. I know because my eldest nearly choked to death on her umbilical cord. Bryan, and other dads, shared the pain of miscarriages and the lack of a community with which to share that pain.

One dad, Steve, shared with me he was the proud father of three children with one dying shortly after birth. His wife and I went to high school together and she introduced us when she heard about my book. They already had an energetic two-year-old when they decided to try for a second child. When they found out they were having twin boys, Steve remembered feeling anxious. Could they handle three? How would their daughter handle two babies instead of just one?

As the pregnancy progressed, warning signs started popping up. One child was hogging the essential nutrients from their twin brother. By the time they reached term, one twin was healthy and fully developed, while the second was malnourished and noticeably smaller. This situation is known as twin-to-twin transfusion syndrome (TTTS). About 25 percent of twins share a common placenta and of those, 10 percent will develop TTTS. That is about six thousand babies a year.

Within hours of both children being born, the younger started getting sick. Doctors determined he would have to be taken to a different hospital for treatment, which meant Steve's newborn sons would be separated by over four hours. None of this had been in their plans to welcome their sons, but it was the reality they were facing.

Sadly, the transfer to a new location didn't help and their youngest died soon after. When I said how sorry I was that he went through this, Steve's response was, "You know, it all happened so fast that we never even got a photo of him. I just took a photo of the clock in the hospital cafeteria. Why would I do that?"

It has been several years since the death of his son, and Steve has finally come to terms with it. He's led support groups through his church and made every second count with his children. As Zaki writes in *The War for Kindness*, this sort of compassion often happens when people endure great hardship. It also manifests in those caregivers and social workers who help bereaved families. There is something about processing grief through supporting others that provides an outlet.

All the dads who shared their stories with me for this chapter buck the "glad, mad, sad" trend. Each, in his own way, stepped up with great courage to share something few have endured. In so doing, we dropped the stereotype of being a lone wolf. The ironic thing is that while our US culture loves a good lone wolf hero (think John McClane in *Die Hard* or John Wick), real life lone wolves in nature don't last long. Wolves are pack animals and take down large prey because they work together. They communicate. They are a team to ensure everyone survives.

A lone wolf doesn't have a pack to ensure their survival, and they don't last long on their own.

THE SIGMA MALE CONSPIRACY

In researching for this chapter, I came across a new term being tossed around social media. Some men are calling themselves "sigma" men or "sigma" males. These are men who choose to live outside of the social order. The term was invented to stand in contrast to "alpha" and "beta," which are common terms used by scientists to denote roles and hierarchy within pack animals. The commonly held misbelief is alpha males gain their position through violence and dominance over other males in the pack.

Yes, there are mating rituals and males do compete for the attention of female members of a pack, but most alpha males gain their position through social relationships and currying favor with others in the pack. Those males who don't fit in are ostracized and left to fend for themselves, find a new tribe, or try to pull a female away from the pack to start their own.

To be clear, in nature, there are no such thing as sigmas. The term was invented in 2010 by an alt-right blogger highlighting individuals like Han Solo and Neo from *The Matrix* as examples. However, it has gained popularity because it provides a "positive" spin on being a loner.

The problem here is men who are declaring themselves as sigmas aren't participating in society. They aren't building strong relationships or empathy. They are remaining stunted and disconnected. Instead of recognizing the pain they are facing or inflicting on others, they turn away from opportunities to be vulnerable and expressive in healthy channels.

This can be seen in the obsession by those engaged on Reddit and other social media threads with characters like Tyler Durden, James Bond, and John Wick. There are also themes of sexual conquest that have no connection to seeing women as people with whom to have relationships.

While many take this entire subject as a giant joke and just something to share via memes, there are young men taking this seriously. And in many ways, the entire structure is a way to reinforce aspects of the "Man Box" just in new packaging and metaphors.

As dads, we cannot shun the relationships we have in our lives. We cannot ignore social order. As servant leaders, it is critical we lean into our social-emotional learning and pave a pathway for our children.

NEXT STEPS

When my daughter was four months old, I took her into the backyard for the first time without snow on the ground. The snow had finally melted, and the ground wasn't a soggy mess. I carried her out to the middle of our yard and carefully placed her bare feet on the grass. At first, she looked around, completely unnerved and confused. She lifted her feet a few times, trusting in me to hold her while she tested her new environment.

Then, ever so quietly, from the back of her throat, a whine grew into a wail. She hated the grass. She became frantic in her efforts to climb back into my arms. I recall simultaneously laughing and having my heart break. As a lover of nature and an avid hiker, could it be that my daughter hated the very thing I loved? The answer was much more simple. She had no concept of grass. She'd been inside or bundled in her car seat and had yet to experience something we take for granted.

I keep this memory with me every time I get frustrated with her. I've had over forty years to figure out life, and I'm still not that great at it. She's eight and despite her attempts at independence, she still needs me from time to time. So I place myself in her shoes and look at the challenges from her perspective. I'm reminded of how big the world truly is and how vulnerable we can feel. More importantly, I'm reminded how much I need to communicate that to her. So in the next chapter, we will dive into the ways we must build communication lines internally and externally.

8

COMMUNICATING AND USING WORDS WHEN NECESSARY

"My first huge accomplishment was knowing the difference between my baby's wet diaper cry and her hungry cry."

—SAM M.

Did you know up to 90 percent of our communication is nonverbal? That means our body language and facial expressions matter far more than the words we say. As humans, we take in important cues and meaning based on these non-verbals. For example, if you see two people leaning toward each other as they are talking, we believe they are having an intimate or heated conversation and don't want to be interrupted. On the flip side, if one person is leaning away from the other, we'd expect they are not interested and looking for an out.

Much of these interpretations are based on cultural norms, but regardless of your culture, the nonverbal components are critical to how we interpret the world around us.

Any new parent will tell you learning their child's babbles and whines is just as critical. For most of the first year of a child's life, they are verbalizing, but actual words don't come around until about one year. Even then, they aren't reciting Shakespeare. Their words are fragmented, and they're still figuring out what things are actually called. My six-year-old still calls earmuffs, "earmugs," and we can't get her to stop!

Many dads I interviewed for this book talk about learning quickly what the difference is between a happy cry, a hungry cry, and a dirty diaper cry. Australian opera singer, Priscilla Dunstan, created an index for parents to help understand baby language. She highlighted five sounds babies make just before crying. These sounds are accompanied by body language and movement and the goal for parents is to pay attention so they can respond appropriately instead of scrambling for an answer.

One dad I interviewed spent hours carefully listening to his child so he could anticipate the cry and save precious time responding to the cry rather than getting frustrated and angry because he couldn't get his child to stop.

Another dad wasn't so lucky. He's a naval officer and when his first child was born, he was completing his certification. Working long hours and studying for his exams made it challenging to get home before his daughter's bedtime. Not wanting to leave his wife to raise the baby alone, he would take the night shift and change his baby and give her bottles of formula. However, he freely admitted he was not nearly as attentive as he needed to be because he was exhausted.

Finally, after a few months, he had a day to be present at home without obligations. His wife took the afternoon to go shopping, and he stayed home. All afternoon, instead of cuddling and having fun, he spent failing time and time again to satisfy his child. What made matters worse was seeing his daughter instantly calm down when his wife returned home. He realized he was absent for so many waking hours that he not only didn't know his daughter's cries, but she didn't know his voice. He'd changed countless diapers during the nighttime hours, but he rarely spoke to her. And in the haze of early morning routines, he was struggling just to get through the day.

So he corrected his behavior as much as he could. He wasn't able to change his long hours right away, but he began singing to her at night to lull her back to sleep and started paying more attention to her cries and nonverbal cues.

As servant leaders, the more we listen, the more we take the cues of our team and our children, the more we can adapt our behavior and address their needs. In doing so, we take the pressure off our partners and take the lead on caring for our families on multiple levels.

THE COMPLICATIONS OF A TECH WORLD

With the rise of smart devices and their near constant stream of information, all of us have a double-edged sword to handle. With smartphones and iPads our distractions are at an all-time high. Chirps and jingles let us know when people (or programs) want our attention. Some are critical, like work emails or our children reaching out to say they need a ride. Others are mere distractions.

As a child, I remember family dinners being sacrosanct. My dad would get home, cook up something, and we'd sit around recounting our days. Often, the only calls that came through were sales calls that we could ignore. Today, parents have to set ground rules for their homes. No cell phones at the table. They place limits on screen time.

In my home, we have a shelf where all electronic devices go. My daughters get screen time to do their homework, but once that is finished, iPads go on the shelf along with my phone. When we first implemented the rule, we all suffered. It was like going through withdrawal because we used my phone to look up recipes for dinner and to play music. After several months, we still struggle with the disconnection, but it is critical for the health of my family.

A 2020 movie called *Save Yourselves!* came out. It's a tiny indie movie without much publicity. It tells a very satirical story of a young couple who keeps falling into the trap of social media and staring at their screens for hours at a time. One weekend, they decide to take a break from technology, the internet, and their phones, and leave for a cabin in the woods. Unbeknownst to them, while in this cabin, strange furry blob-like aliens invade Earth.

At one point, the girlfriend cheats and turns on her phone to find hundreds of voicemails from friends and family. This leads to both making every attempt to understand what has been going on in the alien invasion... which means staring at their cellphones. At the end of the movie, they are deep in the woods trying to escape when their phones distract them, and the strange aliens abduct them.

While this was a satire, how often do we fall into the trap of checking our phones for news headlines or scrolling through Instagram? How often do we go through entire conversations without looking up from our screens or justify looking at our screens to do some research so we can answer our kids' questions?

I know I do, and my kids call me out on it.

They want my attention. They want me to look into their eyes when we speak, and I want them looking at me when I'm giving them instructions. But it isn't on my children to be calling me out. I'm the parent and I have to set the example and provide them with the skills and mindset to flourish... just like you do!

I'M NOT YELLING; THIS IS JUST MY VOICE
John Badalament, Fathering Together's Director of Training and Education, has a booming voice. He's given many presentations and workshops over the years and

has developed a speaking voice that projects and commands attention.

He's also quite tall. So when he speaks, there's a certain level of weight that comes with his words. One time we were in a brainstorming session, and I told him he needed to calm down and stop yelling.

"Brian, I'm not yelling. It's just my voice," he replied, and we all started laughing. Then he continued, "But you know, my daughter tells me the same thing. She thinks I'm yelling at her every time I'm trying to just have a conversation or if I get a little animated on a passionate topic. It is something I have to constantly think about when I talk to her."

I can commiserate with John. My voice gets louder the more passionate I become. I've seen my children jump in shock when I call their name, not out of anger, but because I'm excited to share with them about an upcoming activity or news.

So it is critical to remind ourselves about impact and intent. The intent we have in our messaging is what we can control. The impact we have in our messaging and delivery is something we can't control, or at least not completely. Keeping this in mind as we engage our children can deepen our connection and strengthen our communication.

Dr. Michaelann Doucleff interviewed parents in the Inuit village of Kugaaruk in the Nunavut territory of Canada.

In *Hunt, Gather, Parent*, Dr. Doucleff traveled here because she was always arguing and shouting at her child to behave. At the time of her research, her daughter was at the height of the "three-nager" stage of development.

Having a toddler in the United States is like being a part of a secret club where we all complain and talk about our kid's behavior. I see posts in parenting forums complaining about the terrible twos and three-nager stages. Often these are somewhat in jest with others commenting in commiseration. Some solutions are given and often people take a stance of grin and bear it. But in the workplace, if something's not working right, chances are you find a solution. Chances are you meet with your team leaders and say our system is broken. We're not getting the profit we need. We're not getting the buy in from our investors.

When something's wrong, we identify the problem, research and troubleshoot solutions, and evaluate them. As parents, the same needs to be true. And Dr. Doucleff took her daughter on a whirlwind tour of ancient cultures to find solutions to the breakdown in their relationship. She wanted to know how ancient cultures that still exist in our modern world with all the benefits of technology raise children to be effective and helpful parts of the community.

In Kugaaruk, she found parents who don't get angry or yell at their children. The parents she spoke to explained they expect children to have poor executive function and poor emotional control. So if they yell at their children, all they are doing is role modeling how to be angry and solve problems with anger. But anger is an umbrella emotion. It covers up what is really going on, so if we don't resolve the anger and dig beyond the initial reaction, we won't resolve anything.

Much like our phones being a distraction, the anger and volume of our voices can be a distraction, too.

As I took this in, a memory popped into my mind from the first time I yelled at my daughter. She was about eighteen months old. We're eating breakfast and I gave her some raspberries with her yogurt. Raspberries are tasty. They squish in your fingers, and my daughter and I love them. On this particular morning, she got so excited to eat them, she dropped one on my khaki pants, staining them red.

Without thinking, I shouted at her. I took her out of her seat and put her in timeout. From upstairs, my wife asked if everything was okay. I left her standing in the corner while I ran upstairs to swap my pants and put on some stain remover. I tried explaining what happened to my wife, but the pressure of the clock and daycare and my morning meeting schedule kept ringing in my ears.

Then, I heard my daughter crying downstairs.

And as I pulled on my new pair of pants, I stopped. The reality of the situation slammed into me.

I just yelled at my daughter because of my mistake, not hers.

Like any toddler, it is in their nature to get excited and to get out of control. They haven't learned what "in control" is. They are looking to us to role model and communicate emotional control and healthy communication. And on both fronts, I failed.

For Dr. Doucleff and her experience with the Inuit villagers of Kugaaruk, the lesson goes a step further. We must do more than stop ourselves from reacting in anger. We must also learn to have less anger toward our children.

Our brains are still developing into our twenties. Executive functions start developing just before kindergarten. Between the ages of three and five, our children need us to be at our best to build a scaffold for their success. This happens when we respond with age-appropriate lessons.

COMMUNICATION WITH OUR PARTNERS IS IMPORTANT TOO!

To be effective at servant leadership and remodeling good behavior as dads, we must also think about the communication we have with our partners. As my friend Ted explained, the most important thing he can do to be a good father to his son is to have a strong relationship with his wife.

This can be challenging in the early weeks of parenthood when neither of you are getting adequate sleep and the stresses of managing a new member of the family can put strain everywhere else. However, Eve Rodsky designed a powerful method she dubbed "Fair Play" to help families manage the tasks and chores in their lives.

She developed her system out of necessity. She was leaving on a trip for work and noticed a jacket in the yard and empty beer bottles. Not having time to clean it up, she assumed her husband would see it and clean it up. Yet, the next day when she returned, the mess was still in the yard. Perhaps he had been too busy to notice. Or perhaps, as she would discover, he had gotten distracted by SportsCenter and hadn't gotten to it.

While Eve was traveling, she was also managing schedules for her children, planning playdates, and juggling future work trips. At home, when she walked into the bedroom, she found her husband watching SportsCenter and relaxing on the bed.

In this scenario, you might want to create rationalizations for the husband, and some might even be fair, but the truth is both Eve and her husband were at fault because they had no baseline goals in place. For Eve, she defines this as a Minimum Standard of Care or a shared expectation for what is acceptable in the house and what is not.

In my home, we have a rule that dirty dishes get placed in the dishwasher or cleaned and placed in the drying rack every night. We have routines for book bags and dirty shoes when the kids get home from school. These rules and systems shift and adapt as our children age, but like Eve, my wife and I didn't have many systems in place. As a married couple without kids, we informally divided up the house tasks and made sure things were generally okay. I loved cooking, so I would make dinners, for example.

If communication isn't healthy, if you don't outline expectations, disasters are inevitable. And as a servant leader, our job is to plan for or better yet, avert disaster. Again, easier said than done.

Remember Phil from the "Deep Work" chapter? He and his wife were navigating a newborn in the pandemic without a plan. As I spoke with Phil, he shared his family rarely communicated. He had few memories of his parents setting expectations except for when they divided up chores. So Phil learned the way to show up for a family member is to check off boxes on your to-do list.

As he and his wife stumbled into parenthood, he made sure boxes were checked. He was a skilled manager and executor for this family. However, the heavy work of emotional labor, the planning and ideating on what is best for the family, fell to his wife. Much like Eve, his wife was picking up extra mental work, and Phil was oblivious.

One evening, things came to a head for Phil and his wife. He'd forgotten an item on his checklist. He was quick to apologize, but for his wife, who is more emotionally expressive, she wanted to break things down to understand why he was forgetting. Since Phil's upbringing focused on minimizing conflict and ensuring you get things down without excuses, Phil wasn't prepared for the emotional level of the conversation. He wanted to avoid conflict, correct his mistake, and move on.

For Phil, and so many dads, remember those stay-at-home dads? We often believe we are sharing the work, but in fact, we are simply serving as middle-management. We aren't taking on director level roles or sharing CEO responsibilities with our partners.

Eve will be quick to remind us sharing duties doesn't mean you are both responsible for the same task, but it means ensuring the task lists are divided and everyone shares the responsibility of creating a vision for the future.

This is the second component of Fair Play.

Once a Minimum Standard of Care is established, the tasks are divided and the conception, planning, and execution are developed.

Conception is the first step where you create the vision for what a task entails. For example, I'm in charge of groceries and meals for my home. I took the time to research different apps where my wife and I could share grocery lists instead of writing out what we needed each week. I researched diets and kid-friendly meals so we could prepare meals with minimal arguments from my picky kids.

Next comes Planning. Every Sunday, I map out our list of meals and get buy-in from the kids. On our fridge, we have a whiteboard to highlight important events for the week. It's also where I write down the meals and which kid is getting a school versus home lunch.

Finally, I Execute. I go to the grocery store and check off the items we've purchased. I organize the fridge and throw out expired food or rotten fruit. Then I prep what

I can for the week so should a disaster arise or last-minute change of plans pop up, we can manage. We can be flexible.

Without a plan, without solid communication, this wouldn't be possible.

Servant leaders are rarely the ones who stand up at a podium and make a big speech. Often they are quietly working the background, prepping meals, and mixing lemonade. They are laying the groundwork for success by acknowledging the strengths of those on the team, or in the room. If they don't have powerful communication systems in place, it could all fall apart.

NEXT STEPS

In 2004, I went on a whitewater rafting trip with my dad. After one set of vicious whitewater, our guide told us to sit quietly. As we drifted farther from the rapids, our guide lifted the oars and said, "Look over the edge at the water."

Thousands of tiny bubbles were popping on the surface. The water looked like a pot just before it boils.

"We're over one hundred feet from the rapids, but they are so strong the air they push into the water doesn't have a chance to surface until now."

The experiences we have as children and the experiences we are providing our children can be like rapids. So much is happening that we don't fully appreciate the impact until years or even decades later. And if the rapids are harsh and deadly, like a yelling parent who is just as likely to throw a tantrum as their child, the trauma stays below the surface just like those air bubbles.

As servant leaders, as dads, we should do our best to diminish the rapids and lay a groundwork for open communication so we aren't caught off guard when the air bubbles burst.

Likewise, we must learn to accept our children for who they are and who they will become. In the next chapter, we'll dive into how we can accept ourselves and our children.

PART 4

OTHER-ORIENTED

9

ACCEPTING YOUR KIDS (AND YOURSELF TOO!)

"The one thing I've always wished for my children is for them to feel accepted."

—BRUCE G.

ACCEPTING OUR KIDS

Despite my appreciation for minimalism, I'm a collector. Before everything went digital, I had hundreds of CDs. Books and journals cover one wall of my home office. And, in our storage space, I have boxes of old photos. And to keep myself from verging into hoarder territory, I do not buy extra storage on Google or Apple so that I go through my digital files once a quarter to clear out all the hundreds of photos and videos I don't need.

This past Christmas, I promised my wife I would create an organizational system she could understand should I ever not be available to track down a photo. I did some research to learn the others face similar challenges. Entire blogs and podcasts are dedicated to coaching you through categorizing your digital content. I had my work cut out for me.

As I rewatched old videos and searched photos that jogged long-forgotten memories, a few things dawned on me. First, the subtle shifts from baby-faced, puffy-cheeked infants to kindergartners are incredible to see. Second, the child I saw at six months was completely different from the child at two years and even more foreign than the child I see at eight. Finally, I recalled all the assumptions and goals I had dreamt up for my eldest in those early years of her life. If she opened a book, I jumped on the idea she'd be a world-famous professor. When she took her first steps, naturally that meant she would turn into an Olympic-level sprinter.

When my parents visited for the holidays, I spoke with my dad about this, and per my usual tact, I went about it completely the wrong way.

"Dad, what did you think I would be when I grew up?" I sat at the counter eating cereal while he cleaned up his granddaughter's breakfast dishes.

He pretended to ignore me.

"Dad?"

He sighed, put down the pan he was scrubbing, and replied, "Well, I knew quite a few things I didn't expect of you when you grew up."

My wife let out a guffaw from the living room, and I blushed. I had that coming.

"What's that supposed to mean?"

"Well, it means I knew you were going to make your own life. I just had to do my best to accept it and support you the best I could."

While my father and I spoke of my many, many career ambitions, I thought of the dads I know who were challenged to accept their children for other reasons. In a recent DadChat, we invited Bradford Scott Walton to share his experiences of fatherhood as he raised a child who identifies as trans*. The members who attended all had children of varying ages and identity development.

Most came to listen to Bradford's stories, but when we opened the conversation up for Q and A, the conversation got raw and authentic in no time.

One dad, who refused to be on video, asked in a trembling voice, "I think my daughters is a lesbian, but how do I know?" The question hung in the virtual room.

Bradford responded, "You won't know unless you ask her. How is your relationship?"

The dad didn't respond, so we moved to the next dad on the call. We have a rule during DadChats that everyone is free to take part to the extent they are comfortable, and we don't force people to share if they are not ready.

The next dad, a friend of mine, was eager to share. "My son is only five, but I'm pretty sure he's trans* too. I appreciate hearing your story, Bradford, because it's made me think about how I can show up for him."

Others opened up about raising children with gender identities that didn't fall into a neat binary. Bradford responded with amazing care and respect and guided the conversation to where it needed to go.

By the conclusion, one dad shared what many had been thinking, based on their nodding heads. "I've always considered myself an ally to those who identify within the LGBTQ+ spectrum, but it sure is different when it is your own child."

His name is Matt, and his son is the youngest of three. He's got two older sisters who identify as cisgender girls. As he continued to share his perspective, it was clear to all of us the struggle wasn't whether or not he could accept his child, but how. Having grown up in a more conservative and traditional community, he shared fears about how to explain his child to family members and neighbors.

There were practical questions to consider too, like what clothes should he buy. Matt is a former minister, so there are theological and societal questions as well. For Matt, he consulted scripture and spoke with other ministers from his religious tradition. Regardless of the question that came to his mind, Matt knew he had to find resources and support to navigate this new layer of fatherhood.

The first major challenge he faced on a societal level came on his child's fifth birthday. For most parents, birthdays have enough stress inducements that include themes, food allergies, and safety concerns. That morning, Matt's child said, "I want to wear a dress to my party."

Without hesitation, Matt agreed and helped them pick out their favorite dress. As guests arrived, Matt's child greeted everyone with the unbridled enthusiasm that you would expect from a five-year-old. Their friends danced and ran with the jitters of youth while parents gave greetings and handed over gifts.

No one said anything about the outfit until one mother came up to him saying, "I'm sorry, but we have to leave."

Matt's shoulders tensed, but he remained calm. "Why is that?"

She smiled and said, "My son just told me he wanted to go home and put his dress on. Seeing your son wearing a dress made him jealous."

Matt laughed as he recounted the story in our interview. "I was prepared to get all defensive and judgmental. What a relief that the conversation went in an entirely different direction."

When the mother returned, she found Matt and handed him a pamphlet about a local parent support group as they all navigated raising trans* children together.

While this story had a happy ending for Matt, he still faces challenges from his relatives. Matt's in-laws have referenced a few times wanting to dress their grandchild in more gender-conforming outfits because they don't want their grandchild to be bullied and harassed. Yet, as Matt is quick to point out to them, they are the only ones who have expressed concern thus far.

Isn't it amazing how often we project our own insecurities upon others? Isn't it amazing how our efforts to protect our children can also be a defensive mechanism to uphold a status quo that isn't necessary? Matt's son wants to wear a dress. So what?

Research from the Trevor Project, a worldwide suicide prevention and crisis intervention organization for LGBTQ young people, looked at gender-affirming hormone therapy and other forms of support for trans* children. They found strong links between affirming attitudes and lower rates of depression, suicidal thoughts, and suicide attempts by young people.

While Matt's child is still very young, Dan's child is fifteen and when they turned fourteen, they announced they thought they were a lesbian. Then after some exploration, thought that perhaps they were non-binary, and only recently decided perhaps trans* was the best fit term for their gender identity.

I've known Dan through the entire journey, and he has expressed on numerous occasions how challenging it has been to watch their child process all this information. In our last conversation, which was specifically around this book, he shared, "As much as I've struggled to come to terms with this past year, I can't imagine what my child is going through. I've done my best to support them, but I still have so much to learn."

Dan's family lives in a larger town in Georgia and they've connected with PFLAG, an LGBTQ+ organization focused on supporting people, their parents, families, and allies. Through the local chapter, Dan and his wife have met with other parents and learned how to be stronger allies and parents for their child, who is in transition as well as their younger child who is cisgender, but much younger and needing help to process the change taking place in their family as well.

For Dan, one of the biggest challenges to accept was his son renaming himself. As Dan put it, "The first gift you give to your child is their name. So when he wanted to change his name, I really struggled. Then when he said he wanted his name to be Shark, I put my foot down. That was a hard conversation, but we finally came around to a name that made sense and reflected his true nature."

ACCEPTING OURSELVES
Acceptance is a two-way street. By this I mean we have to accept our children for who they will become and we need to accept ourselves for who we are. The conversation with my dad was a reminder of that for me and when I spoke with Bruce, one of my dad's best friends, he hammered home this lesson.

Bruce's daughter and I attended three-year-old preschool together, and our families became close friends. Like my dad's friend Ross, Bruce became another father figure to me, and I spent many weekends sitting on his couch watching golf while his daughters and my sister played.

When I was in seventh grade, his firstborn died in a terrible car accident, and it shook all of us. His son was the oldest out of all us kids, and we all looked to him as an older brother. I still remember my dad holding Bruce as he sobbed. I was twelve and had never seen my dad, or Bruce, be so emotional. Bruce's daughter, my friend, was in shock on the couch with paramedics checking on her.

And as terrible as that night was for everyone, another revelation about Bruce was awaiting me years later.

Shortly after turning fifty, Bruce found his birth parents. In an ironic twist of fate, they lived just one town over, and his birth mother died a year before Bruce found her.

When I interviewed Bruce, he told me, "Brian, I've never wanted to be famous. I've never dreamt big dreams for myself or my kids. I just wanted them, and you and your sister too, to be happy. And most of all, I wanted you all to feel accepted. I never felt accepted."

This admission to me broke my heart. Here was a father figure who had helped to define fatherhood for me. I had never known he was adopted. No one really talked about it. Yet, throughout our interview, being an orphan grounded his worldview and his experiences in life.

To have him share such a deeply personal thing left me speechless. Later in the day, when my girls came home from school, I picked them up, hugged them, and didn't let them go for quite a while.

The truth is you can't hug someone long enough to make them feel accepted. But what you can do is show up, listen to them, and appreciate all they are going through. Bruce lost a son and spent the majority of his life without knowing his birth parents. Yet, I've felt nothing less than acceptance from him.

The same is true with another dad I met through this book project.

On Danny's fourth birthday, he proclaimed, "I'm going to be married and have ten children when I turn eighteen."

His parents nodded and smiled, like any parent would, but then they got divorced when he was eight. His mom remarried a couple years after that, and his stepdad turned out to be abusive while his biological dad remained fairly absent. Despite these challenges, Danny never gave up on his dream.

When he turned eighteen, he had a girlfriend who he was crazy about, and called up his dad.

When his dad picked up, he asked, "So, you're getting married?"

"How did you know?" Danny replied.

"Because you are eighteen. You were so sincere when you were four, that I've been expecting this phone call ever since."

True to his word, Danny married at eighteen and got divorced a few months later. The children would have to wait. But Danny was persistent and dedicated to fulfilling his dream. Soon he met another woman and got married to her.

But again, the relationship ended in divorce. Danny tried to connect and be present to both his ex-wives, but something was blocking him from a deeper level of intimacy. His past got in the way of his abilities to connect and build a healthy marriage, but he hadn't realized how impactful the abuse had been on him.

After his second marriage, Danny had doubts about his dream of fatherhood. Maybe his proclamation would amount to a childish flight of fancy.

However, Danny wasn't ready to completely give up hope. Throughout his twenties and his two failed marriages, Danny had received a diagnosis that he was ADHD and bipolar. He took his medications, but there was still something wrong. He struggled to find real intimacy and connection, not just with his ex-wives, but friendships too. So he went back to therapy for a fresh take on his situation.

Finally, in his mid-thirties, his doctor diagnosed him with PTSD stemming from the years of abuse from his stepfather. With this diagnosis, articles, and a workbook,

Danny realized why he would hyperventilate and have anxiety attacks. He started looking for signs that could trigger an attack or bring out his anger in unhealthy ways.

Amid all this, he met Angela. She encouraged and supported his journey to recovery. She wanted kids too, maybe not ten, but definitely a few. Much like Ted and his wife Franzi, she understood a healthy marriage was the essential foundation for having children. So together, they worked on communication, trust, and intimacy.

When Angela told Danny they were going to have a baby, she also said she didn't want to give up on her career. Danny agreed.

So at dinner one evening, a new challenge arose.

He stated, "I always saw my kids having a stay-at-home parent."

Angela smiled. "I did too. So, when are you going to quit your job?"

Danny was taken aback. What was she talking about? "Why am I going to be the stay-at-home parent?"

"If you want our kids to have a stay-at-home parent, then you should be the stay-at-home parent."

After a second to process what Angela had just said, Danny realized he wasn't just okay with being an at-home dad, he was excited about it.

Fifteen years later, he's still excited about it and has turned that excitement into leadership with the National At-Home Dad Network and a weekly mental health discussion group for dads dealing with PTSD.

As he said to me during the interview, "I knew I needed help with my PTSD and abuse, but every group I found for sexual abuse support was designed for women. My presence would not help those women in their recovery because most of them had husbands or other men abuse them. I didn't want to be a reminder or an obstacle to their recovery, but I knew I needed support. So I spoke with one facilitator who advised me to start my own group."

Shortly after the pandemic began, Danny started posting on social media feeds with invitations to join him. His first weekly meeting had a few participants, and with each subsequent week, more dads began attending. Word had spread, and Danny realized he wasn't alone.

After a few months, he had a core group of supporters joining him on Zoom to share their experiences of abuse and other forms of trauma. Danny accepts the gifts that have been granted to him in life and while he would never wish abuse upon his younger self, he is learning to use his experiences to help others.

As a former campus minister, I worked with dozens of students who came to college to get a degree their parents wanted for them. I remember taking a student to lunch and she broke down into tears because her parents expected her to go on to medical school and become a doctor. Anything else would be a waste of everyone's time.

The problem is she hated the idea of being a doctor. She loved her business classes, and creating a business plan and budget made so much more sense to her than studying medical reports and memorizing drugs and their side effects. I worked with her to create a plan to speak with her parents about going into hospital administration. She would combine her talents and her parents' desires.

Recently, I ran into her at LaGuardia Airport. I had my daughter with me and as we entered the boarding area, I saw her on the phone. She turned toward me, and her jaw dropped in surprise. She ended the call and gave me a bear hug.

"So, what are you doing with your life?" I asked.

She smiled and said, "I'm a hospital administrator. The plan you and I created went over well with my parents and I'm following my dream."

Not all children find such healthy solutions. The Trevor Project pulls together ample data sets to highlight the painful reality of parental rejection on their kids. Research highlights that a third of children will be accepted, a third rejected, and another third never disclose their LGBTQ identity. Of those young adults who report parental rejection, they are eight times more likely to attempt suicide and six times more likely to report high levels of depression.

NEXT STEPS

As fathers, and as servant leaders, we have an opportunity to change the narrative. We can see children's abilities to express and define themselves as a positive thing, not a negative thing. Looking back to Dr. Doucleff's interviews with traditional cultures, we can recognize the gift our children bring into our lives and support them in their journey of self-expression rather than forcing them to conform to systems that work to harm them and us.

As bell hooks points out in *The Will to Change*, she always expected her father to control her life. The bigger pain was watching her caring and expressive brother become a cruel teenage boy in an attempt to be a man. Her brother smothered his dreams and identity to conform to what her father and their culture demanded of him.

As a servant leader to my children, I cringe knowing how many children won't meet their potential. As more organizations step up like PFLAG and Trevor Project, and as more parents accept their children for who they are and not force them into who they believe their children to be, I'm hopeful for the future.

One way dads can do this is by never forgetting the importance of learning. In the next chapter, we'll spell out how you can take steps to be a life-long learner.

PART 5

ADVOCACY

10

CULTIVATING A LEARNING MINDSET

"My daughters gave me the gray hairs and the wisdom to go along with it. Man, they push my boundaries, but they're making me a better dad too."

—CURTIS W.

On a recent trip with my daughters, I had a chance to pause and appreciate the wonders around me. We had planned to go to Disney World as a family to escape the cold of a Chicago winter. But, with the surge of cases with Omicron, we had to postpone.

With our week up for grabs, I suggested a hike at nearby Fort Sheridan. The former military base had been turned into a nature preserve with a few miles of hiking trails and beautiful views of Lake Michigan. The girls were hesitant given the cold, so I sweetened the deal with the promise of hot chocolate afterward.

We met up with some friends who also have two daughters who needed some outdoor adventures to burn off energy. With the car loaded down with extra winter gear, snacks, and a thermos of hot chocolate, we drove to meet them.

As we made our way from the parking lot toward the scenic outlook, we spied a pond that had frozen over. Fox prints cut through a thin layer of fresh snow across the pond. I looked at the other dad with a smile. I think my daughter saw me because she immediately asked to go out onto the ice.

He stepped onto the ice first to test its thickness and ensure our daughters' safety. But I could tell just standing on the shore we had nothing to fear.

Within minutes, we were slipping and sliding back and forth across the pond. The girls attempted triple axels and salchows while I attempted to point out the trapped bubbles of air. I caught their attention for a few minutes to have the impromptu science lesson before they were off again. They forgot about the frigid air and the complaints from the hike over. Before we knew it, what had meant to be a thirty-minute hike turned into a two-hour adventure.

My daughters filled the drive home with questions where hot chocolate awaited us.

"How did the bubbles form again?"

"Why were there so many?"

"What else could be frozen in the ice?"

"How did the fish survive?"

Their questions were endless and my ability to answer them without the help of Google became strained. I definitely made up a few answers. It was a marvelous day.

While the hike created new learning opportunities for my daughters, it created opportunities for me, too. At the conclusion of 2021, I was going one thousand miles a minute to raise funds, implement strategies for 2022, and ensure my organization, Fathering Together, kept growing. In the process, I nearly forgot the promises I had made to my daughter when she yelled at me for not being a good dad.

During the hike and our impromptu ice-skating competition, it reminded me of how important it was for me to continue to learn and grow alongside them. Their minds are starving for information. They consume information at an ever-expanding rate and that isn't even considering the massive amount of data available to them online compared to our childhoods.

So I made another promise to them. My word for 2022 would be to "decelerate." It became my word because I realized I kept accelerating on an empty tank and eventually I was going to hit a wall. I've hit walls before; I've run out of gas, and it isn't healthy or helpful. Furthermore, decelerating doesn't mean you aren't progressing. It just means you aren't willing to sacrifice your health or your relationship in the process.

The days after the hike, I fought against placing my kids in front of a screen while I answered emails and wrote up reports. I could have justified that by giving them a documentary or some other educational show, but the emails weren't as critical as fresh air and exploring another part of our community we had yet to explore.

So how do you appreciate the wonder around you? How do you cultivate a dad-mindset enriched by a love of learning?

A DAD'S INSPIRATION
For Victor Aragon, he looks to his son. Victor grew up quiet and shy and the youngest out of all his cousins. His son is in a similar position. He's the youngest and often is left behind when his big sister goes out to play with neighbors, and they don't live near extended family, so any playdates with cousins take effort, especially in the midst of the pandemic.

One difference between Victor and his son is that his son has seizures. These seizures have made it difficult for his son to engage with friends at school. But, unlike Victor, who turned to video games and science fiction to combat being left out on activities, his son took to gymnastics.

With a few years under his belt, he still makes mistakes and fails during practice when trying new routines. Victor goes to every practice and watches from the stands. He's noticed a pattern. His son will fall, sometimes really hard, and then walk away from the apparatus. He'll stand quietly with his back to the team and coaches. Then he'll come back and attempt the routine again.

After practice one day, Victor approached his son's coach to see what he could do to help his son. The coach explained Victor's son will cry and get really tough on himself when he walks away from the team. The coach had learned to give the boy a few minutes alone to calm himself and refocus. So he asked Victor to encourage his son and cultivate the intrinsic motivation to keep going at gymnastics.

What Victor also took away from the experience was a bit of jealousy toward his son. As Victor told me, "I have plenty of days when I want to give up, especially when my job isn't the best. I want to just quit. But my son doesn't quit. He keeps going, so I have to do the same."

Then last year, Victor and his son committed to doing a Spartan Race together. A Spartan Race is a three-mile (or much longer) distance with obstacles and challenge elements peppered throughout. Participants face mud pits, lugging sandbags back and forth, and climbing towers before crossing the finish line. Victor wasn't sure his son would be up for it when he suggested the activity. But his son couldn't wait.

"For me, I had more fun training with him and running alongside him as we conquered each element. Seeing him persevere and fight for victory was one of my proudest moments." Victor had tears in his eyes as he revisited the memories.

While Victor's stories are a lesson in resilience, they are also a lesson in lifelong "learnership." In Victor's case, he's learned to see his son as a teacher for him. Often, we fall into the trap of thinking we have to know everything and teach our children how to survive. But educators like Paulo Freire and organizations like Chicago Scholars have long understood students and children have the power to educate adults.

Paulo Freire wrote *Pedagogy of the Oppressed* in response to a growing sense of fear and disenfranchisement of Brazilian children. Because of their fear, they could not envision a world that could be. Instead, they envisioned a world as it is and no effort on their part could change that. As an educator, this pained Freire. For him, the point of education is to empower us to make changes and have the skills and knowledge to do it.

Thus, Freire wrote against the "banking system" of education that assumed "knowledge is a gift bestowed by those who consider themselves knowledgeable upon those whom they consider to know nothing." In this way, students store knowledge rather than "develop the critical consciousness which would result from their intervention in the world as transformers of that world."

For Freire, his new method saw teachers as educators. He called it problem-posing education, where "people develop their power to perceive critically the way they exist in the world with which and in which they find themselves; they come to see the world not as a status reality, but as a reality in process, in transformation."

This philosophical approach has been used by many educators in higher education and in organizations like the Chicago Scholars Foundation. Their mission is to "select, train, and mentor academically ambitious students from under-resourced communities to complete college and become the next generation of leaders who will transform their neighborhoods and our city."

The students who enter programs with the Chicago Scholars Foundation gain access to mentors from professional sectors and peers who have gone through the program before them. In this way, they have multiple opportunities to find role models and access to growth. In the twenty-five years of their existence, many of their scholars have gone on to be civic and business leaders, and just as importantly, paved the way for their younger siblings and relatives to follow in their footsteps.

Not surprisingly, because they focus solely on the children, they offer limited support for parents of their scholars, but they have noticed a trend that younger siblings apply when they see their older siblings' success. They've also seen more involvement from the parents. This shows up as parents calling in with support questions and demonstrating a desire to help their children reach success. This desire by the parents to ensure their children's success is at the heart of being a servant leader.

CREATE OPPORTUNITIES

When we first told my in-laws we were going to be parents, I pulled my father-in-law to the side. I asked him if he had any tips or strategies to pass on to me.

He responded, "Just make sure you create opportunities for your child to be exposed to everything. That's what I did."

My father-in-law worked in radio and telecommunications for decades. Often, this work translated to leaving work before 5:00 a.m. so he could get to the studio for the morning reports. Other days, it meant returning home just before bed to tuck in his kids. But my father-in-law is also an entrepreneur and tinkerer.

When I first met my wife, she had a first-aid kit in her car plus a bag with an emergency light, tools, and coveralls. She told me they were just one of her father's many inventions and side hustles. But his true love is his Triumph. He'd built a detached garage to hold three of them. One was being built, one was his touring car, and the last one was for parts.

Just like with his daughter, my wife, whenever my daughters visit, he finds ways to bring them into the garage to have them help and learn about car maintenance. My wife will freely admit she can't remember half the lessons he taught her, but she does know her way around a car. For my father-in-law, it wasn't just that he wanted her to be knowledgeable. He wanted her to fall in love with learning so she would ask questions and probe deeper into anything she came into contact with.

For my wife, this translated to being a three-sport athlete with an avid passion for running. So one year, my father-in-law committed to running a 5K fun-run with her. He struggled every step of the way, but he crossed the finish line.

To this day, he'll bring up this story to prove he was once athletic. For me, though, the lesson is we must learn alongside our children and show them education doesn't end upon graduation.

NEXT STEPS

In my senior year of high school, I took AP Calculus. Our teacher, Mr. Chastain, opened the class on the first day by telling us what we learn in this class will tell us how to pick the best seat in a movie theater. We all laughed, but a few weeks later, we did. He was true to his word.

Until that point, I'd always just enjoyed learning for the sake of learning. I'd never been pushed to apply my knowledge, or at least, I was never self-aware enough to realize all the tests and all the real-world challenges my dad put forward to me in our home projects were opportunities to apply my knowledge.

Now, as a dad, I'm constantly thinking about it and how to get my daughters to apply their knowledge. In the next two chapters, we'll dive into advocacy and how dads are using their knowledge to advocate for change on multiple fronts.

11

BECOMING AN ALLY

"As dads, we have an important role to play and oftentimes, we don't take the chance. But we can't shy away from those changes."

—CRAIG P.

"What did you think of the role play in class today?" my friend, Ryan, asked me.

"You mean when Todd wore a dress and spoke in falsetto to portray a gay man?" I clarified.

"Yes, exactly that." My friend identifies as a gay man, and I heard him gasp during the role play. I felt his anger radiate from him during the exercise.

"I thought it was ridiculous, and I know Todd is better than that," I started, but my friend cut me off.

"Brian, I consider you a friend and an ally, but this is where you really need to step up. Todd won't hear me tell him his portrayal of a gay man was offensive. But he will listen to you. You are his friend, so I need you to speak for me. This is what being an ally means."

Ryan and I were first-year graduate students to become higher education administrators. This particular class was on multiculturalism, and one assignment was to role play how to address difficult topics with students.

I spoke with Todd. I went on to speak with dozens of Todds, but there will always be more.

And there will always be guys like Andrew, who came up to our White Ribbon Campaign table and asked what we were doing.

One of my student leaders explained, "The White Ribbon Campaign is a call to men to stop doing violence toward women and girls. We're asking people to wear a white ribbon to show our solidarity."

"Even if they hit us first?" Andrew laughed and my student leader chuckled, and I lost it. I'd already had a long day of debating with students. Unfortunately, Andrew's comment was the last straw for me that day.

I stepped in and, with a little too much passion, explained to Andrew how inappropriate it was and how we couldn't give him a white ribbon. In this situation, I lost an opportunity to get through to Andrew because I shamed him rather than invited him into a deeper relationship.

I learned a lot from my interaction with Andrew and Todd. Over the next fifteen years, I'd struggle with maintaining my ally status, but having daughters brought that title into an entirely new light.

CHANGING YOUR PERSPECTIVE

The rest of this chapter will continue into chapter twelve. In this chapter, I'll be focusing on what it means to become an ally for your family and community. Much like becoming a parent, it takes a lot of deep work to recognize the systems that aren't working and how you may or may not benefit from them. Once this is done, you can begin to dismantle and create positive change, which we'll cover in the next chapter. Because of the topics covered in my interviews with dads, I'll be using gender to ground the conversation in this chapter and race to ground the next chapter.

I shared my daughter's birth story in chapter one, but what I left out were the thoughts about preparing my daughter for our world where I know women who carry mace or hold her car keys as a weapon when they walk home at night.

Immediately, I felt an obligation to end systems of oppression that awaited my daughter, and my second daughter, who would come in another two and a half years. I reconnected with men who were advocating for gender equitable systems and training allies to end gender-based violence.

Fellow dad and author, Mike Adamick, summed it up beautifully in his book *Raising Empowered Daughters*, where he wrote, "I'm not sure we do a good job preparing our children for a world that still treats our daughters as second-class citizens and our sons as angry, entitled automatons."

I couldn't agree more. So I started over in becoming an ally. I retraced my steps to recognize I'm not perfect, but

I do hold a lot of privilege in our society. I did some deep work to see how my privilege plays out in my relationships at home and in the workplace. And I turned my learning mindset back on and dove into the literature and advocacy spaces.

For dads who want to become an ally for their children, this is where it starts. You can't be an ally for something if you know nothing about the oppressed group for whom you want to advocate. This educational process isn't just reading books and articles, but humbling yourself to sit quietly and listen to their stories.

Just like we do as dads when listening to our children, we have to place ourselves in the shoes of others and recognize their experience. Since I am a dad with two daughters, the easiest place for me to start was understanding the world my daughters would face.

THE PROBLEM

Here's the stark reality: One in three women will face sexual violence in their lifetime, according to the latest UN report. Other research gathered by RAINN (the Rape, Abuse & Incest National Network) points to one in six women being raped during college. It isn't just women and girls, though. Boys and men are also victims and survivors of sexual assault.

What is worse is most of these numbers are not accurate because there is massive under-reporting of these numbers. When we meet women, who step forward with doubt and suspicion, or they are treated like they should be held responsible as well, it sends a signal that keeps others from reporting. For example, there is an international blue jeans day on April 26 because a woman wore tight blue jeans, and a man raped her. The judge didn't convict the man because he assumed she must have helped him remove her clothes, thus granting consent.

Compounding this was a 2015 rape case where a Stanford swimmer attempted to rape an unconscious woman. The judge gave him a reduced sentence because he didn't want his future ruined. The extremely lenient sentence sends a message to our daughters they are second-class citizens. But as dads, we know our children are not second class. We see the light they bring to the world. So why would we settle?

One dad who doesn't settle is Craig Parks.

Craig is a former camp counselor, turned musician, and has added "amazing dad" to his resume. His first child was born nearly twenty years ago. He identifies on the autism spectrum and is an aspiring DJ. His second child, a girl, is eight. Craig has faced his fair share of challenges in his life while raising two children, but he wouldn't change it for the world.

I met Craig in a Clubhouse room focused on parenting. Early in the COVID-19 pandemic, he and his daughter had taken to Facebook to host live concerts to help everyone get through the challenges of daily life. He told the room how it had been a transformation for his relationship with his daughter. I instantly liked him.

A few days later, we found time to connect over the phone and he shared how he hadn't been sure about fatherhood as a teenager. He knew it was an expectation from his family, but he was busy being a kid and striving to be a musician.

His drive to be a musician led him to serve at his local synagogue as a musical director. This, in turn, led to working as a camp counselor during the summer months. Each summer, he'd play music, lead prayers, and help his students figure out life.

Then one summer after he had been promoted to Director for Youth Programming, he met Samantha. He called her into his office to clarify a rumor that was going around. Craig had heard she had performed oral sex with one of the male campers. When he brought up the rumor, she got defensive.

"Am I going to get expelled?" she asked.

"No!" Craig replied.

"Are you going to tell my parents?" She followed as tears ran down her cheeks.

Craig took a different approach and asked, "Why are you engaging in this type of activity with them?"

"Because the boys like it," she replied.

"Do you like it?" he asked.

"I don't know. I guess it is a way for them to like me," she answered.

Her response stunned him. Over the years, Craig had lots of kids come through his programs with stories of abandonment and emotional distance from their fathers. He'd dealt with eating disorders and troublemakers who lashed out in anger instead of recognizing their emotions, but he hadn't faced a situation like this. He hadn't faced a situation of a girl choosing to be treated as an object rather than a person, nor had he quite realized that her self-worth was wrapped up in this understanding.

When he met with the boy who received the oral sex, he took a compassionate approach. He knew him to be a role model to other kids at the camp, so he asked him, "Do you know anything about this other camper? Like her family situation, or like if there's any abuse in her background?"

"No, why?" the boy answered.

"Well, I'm just trying to see if you know her or if this was just a random hookup. Because she's a human being with feelings and emotions, and I bet she's struggling right now."

"I never thought of it that way."

As Craig continued to speak with the boy, he became clear that no one had ever spoken to the boy about sex and sexuality or relationships. In the boy's ignorance, he'd just seen an opportunity to hook up. But when faced with the humanity of the other camper, the boy realized the seriousness of the situation.

After the experience, Craig realized his preparation as a camp counselor had been lacking in a few key areas. He'd studied adolescent development and social pressures teenagers face, but he wasn't as aware of gender-based violence and its many complex forms. So he took time to educate himself so should another incident arise, he'd be prepared for it. And better yet, he ensured that the following year; they incorporated training for the other counselors about how to handle situations like this too.

It isn't just youth summer campers who need allyship. It happens in the offices and workplaces all the time too. Drs. David Smith and Brad Johnson wrote *Good Guys* to draw attention to the ways men can be allies for women in Corporate America. Their advice goes far beyond what Craig had to deal with.

First, they highlight the disparity between the roles of men and women in the executive level. It wasn't until the 1970s a woman sat in the CEO chair of a Fortune 500 company. Even at the time of writing this book, only forty-one of the Fortune 500 companies have women CEOs.

Second, the lack of paid parental leave creates challenges for parents to live an integrated life. Women are expected to take leave, and many don't return to the workplace, whereas men don't take parental leave and then feel challenged to connect with their kids at home.

According to a recent study by the Mayo Clinic, half of women who take maternity leave don't return to their jobs. While more corporations are including parental leave, most don't provide return-to-work programs. This is changing with organizations like Mindful Return founded by Lori Mihalich-Levin. Her company offers courses and HR support to parents and companies alike to help bring people back to the workforce. Another nonprofit organization, Path Forward, founded by Tami Forman, works with individuals to find new careers after being out of the workforce. They also work with companies to find those individuals with gaps in their resume.

The pandemic has created opportunities for companies to reimagine the workforce, but it will take more than moms and dads speaking up to make these changes. It will take a shift in our language and mindset as fathers and servant leaders to do this.

This is a lot to process, and in conversations I've had with other dads, the change that needs to happen can feel immense. But let's realize for a moment that we stand at the top of the problem. Many of us can look down upon the problem and see the system benefits us. While there are dads who have to battle in court for custody and while men are victims of sexual assault, the vast majority of our systems (in the US) are designed to keep men in positions of power and control.

I never really accepted this until I attended a workshop with Paul Kivel. Paul Kivel is an educator, writer, and activist who has been leading workshops, establishing programs, and empowering people to rethink systems of violence longer than I've been alive. He co-founded the Oakland Men's Project in 1979 to have men reimagine our role in gender-based violence. In 2008, in a community center in Seattle, he pulled up a slide with a list of "powerful groups" on one side and "less powerful groups" on the other. At the time, I wasn't rich or a boss, but every other word under "powerful" defined who I was.

He went on to ask questions like, "Who has always seen someone like them reporting the news?" and "Who has someone in Congress that looks like them?" With each question, his point hit home harder and harder.

So, yes, the challenge is immense, but aren't our children worth it? Don't you want a world that accepts and treats your child with as much dignity and respect as they deserve?

So let's break down a few actions that we, as dads, can do.

ACTION STEPS

REFRAME OUR LANGUAGE
Start by reframing the narrative of gender-based violence. More often than not, we hear the passive voice of "she was raped or assaulted," but what we need to say is that someone raped her. Someone chose to take action against a woman or girl. Jackson Katz, another long-time advocate and producer of *Tough Guise* and author of *The Macho*

Paradox, highlights our use of language. The passive voice removes the perpetrator from responsibility and shifts it to the victim, or survivor, of the act.

Second, we need to stop joking about it. Early in the formation of our Dads with Daughters community, there would be new members posting memes with "rules for dating my daughter." Most of these highlighted just one: "Don't!" There'd be others who would post comments about buying a gun and locking the doors. This assumes two things, and neither is good:

It assumes your daughter is helpless and needs your protection.

It assumes every boy is out to get her.

When we would remove these posts, other members would get angry and say it was posted as a joke. Yet, some of those same dads I would see post in other dad forums saying such things as "she had it coming."

I don't know about you, but I was raised to be non-violent and no matter what the other person did, they didn't deserve to be assaulted by me.

Remember, you don't have to raise your son to be a rapist and you don't have to raise your daughter to be a helpless victim. You can raise both to be empowered and make healthy choices and lead with relationship, like Craig did with the boy camper.

Another way this "joking" shows up is in the normalization of female victimization in our media. A classic example is shown by the *Looney Tunes* character: Pepe Le Pew. I was never a huge fan of *Looney Tunes*, but that's what was on during Saturday mornings. So of course, I watched them religiously with my sister. It wasn't until graduate school that I realized how awful and problematic his character was. To be clear, Pepe Le Pew is a stalker and rapist. He'll stop at nothing to get the female character in every cartoon. Even after she repeatedly tells him she is not interested, he ignores all her signs.

Some might say, "it is just a cartoon" and "don't take it so seriously." But remember the stats from the start of this chapter? One in three women will face sexual assault in their lifetime. We get to that statistic because we make it funny to laugh at women's pain.

And what of the girls who watched those cartoons? What impact was it having on my sister who, every Saturday morning, was reminded her voice, her bodily autonomy, and her agency to determine who and what she wanted in life would come second to a man's carnal desires?

Third, let's talk about language and body parts. As dads, we must normalize the female body by using correct terminology. Get comfortable saying terms like vulva and vagina and labia majora. Understand the uterus is where the baby develops when your wife is pregnant. Just as important, talk about having a penis and testicles, because if you have a daughter, she is going to be very curious.

This curiosity is not a bad thing and should not be shamed. Remember, they are little sponges and soak up all the information they can. They want to understand the world around them and why daddy pees standing up and why they can't. We only make it "weird" and uncomfortable if we are insecure about it.

ALLYSHIP IN THE WORKPLACE

Second, let's talk about the workplace and how to advocate for change.

David Smith and Brad Johnson authored *Athena Rising* and *Good Guys*. In their first book, *Athena Rising*, they lay out strategies for men to mentor women. They challenged men to be more inclusive in their role as mentors and provide opportunities for women to gain access to spaces that were previously (but unspoken) men only. In their second, *Good Guys*, they expand their argument and provide specific tasks men can do to create more inclusive workplaces.

When I spoke with David Smith about this, his "why" stemmed from the challenge he and his wife went through when his kids were young. Being in the US Navy meant they had little expendable income and lots of demands on his time. He saw his wife struggle to keep things together in the home and the imbalance of gender expectations.

Concurrently with that, he remembered how important it was to meet up with other dads to support one another in fatherhood. They would go on group playdates and sit around a table in a coffee shop and discuss how they could be better and stronger role models for their children and more supportive husbands for their wives. For David, this translated into an understanding that if we aren't able to shift our mindsets to becoming servant leaders and advocates in the home, we won't be successful in the workplace.

Currently, David and Brad work with companies to develop male ally communities that focus on organizational change from the top down. When they speak with a company, a senior leader, preferably someone at the C-Suite level, must endorse and provide an opening address for the day. From there, they focus on emotional intelligence, define terms like accountability and transparency while establishing a community of allies to cultivate connection and collaboration.

Much like I shared in the chapter on empathy, allyship comes down to relationships and placing yourself into the shoes of those with whom you want to elevate. But, it also means to be proactive in the desire for change. We need to shift from an ally, who gives support, to one who engages in the ongoing work to dismantle, reimagine, and build a new structure that provides opportunities for our children to thrive.

NEXT STEPS
In the next chapter, I'll dive further into this term as an aspect of the fatherhood mindset, but to provide one

illustration, you need to meet Angus. Angus is a former coffee house minister who organized concerts before having a personal and professional breakdown. In this breakdown, he got divorced, lost his job, and found himself at a loss. Then he met his second wife, remarried, and found new purpose in helping men achieve their goals.

Then in the summer of 2020, he had another awakening. His adopted daughter is a woman of color. After George Floyd's murder, the two of them sat down to discuss the impact of the moment on their family. They attended a protest together because he wanted to support her, but as they debriefed the experience, he continued to make colorblind comments. She called him out on each one. But what struck him the hardest was her admission she was anxious around him because of those comments.

So he shifted. He realized he was part of the problem and researched how to remove problematic language from his vocabulary. He read books like Ibram Kendi's *How to Be an Anti-Racist* and Dorothy Roberts' *Fatal Invention*. By doing so, Angus showed his oldest daughter he wasn't just going to perform allyship, he was going to act on it too. For his younger children, this manifested in removing them from their school environment and finding home schooling materials that align with being a co-conspirator. Their new curriculum incorporates more diversity and a richer history that acknowledges past pain and injustices.

12

ADVOCATING
FOR CHANGE

"I'm preparing my daughter to be a counter narrative for what people think about black girls."

—TIM W.

"Don't turn it down, Dad!" my six-year-old demands from the backseat. We're headed to a nearby park to go for a hike, and we had been listening to *Wait Wait... Don't Tell Me!* on NPR. At its conclusion, I had planned on switching to music, but a report on George Floyd's murder popped up.

It's the summer of 2020 and we're deep into the pandemic and the anxiety of the impending presidential elections. My wife and I were trying to maintain a sense of order in our lives, so taking the girls on errands where we didn't have to leave the car and hikes in nearby forest preserves allowed for breaks from our house.

After the news report ended, I changed the channel and asked, "Do you have any questions about what you heard?"

She replied with questions like, "What's a protest?" and "Are we going to join them?" and finally, "Why would the police murder someone?"

All her questions were honest and real, and I wasn't as prepared as I should have been. So I did my best to answer her. I explained the US Constitution and the Bill of Rights that protected our freedom of speech and assembly. I tried explaining about the important work of caring for those in our community and standing up for what is right. I also explained people make mistakes and sometimes those mistakes lead to people dying.

But for my daughter, all she heard was a police officer killed a black man and her best friend is black.

So, her next question was, "Will Mr. Smith kill my friend someday?"

We had just pulled into the parking lot of the forest preserve for our hike, but it was the last thing from my mind. How was I going to explain this?

My friends, who identify as African American or Black, know how to explain this. Throughout that summer, they shared with me the stories of "the Talk" they have with their children. "The Talk" is about how to hold yourself in a crowded space. How to make yourself look small if you're too tall as a Black man, so you aren't considered a threat to a white woman. How to talk and handle yourself around police officers so you weren't shot and murdered. In Ibram Kendi's book *How to Be an Anti-Racist,* he outlines "the Talk" from his own experiences.

For Ibram and other dads of color, "the Talk" is not an option. It is survival.

On that Saturday afternoon hike, I was keenly aware of the option I had to push the talk to another day, because I felt my daughter was too young to deal with those issues. I could have easily shifted the conversation to a cartoon or thinking about a gift for her sister's upcoming fourth birthday. As a white dad, I stood in a place of privilege, but I also knew my daughter wouldn't let me change the topic. When her mind was set on something, nothing could distract her.

So as we walked, I used strategies from Ibram Kendi's book and others to help my daughter understand the context of race in the United States. To be anti-racist, we have to have these conversations. We cannot leave them to people of color to have with their children.

Just as I shared in the previous chapter with the dark reality of gender-based violence at my daughter's birth, I never had thoughts about her skin color. Again, I stood in a position of privilege, but I should have. I should have recognized that the fears I had for her gender were the same fears as my fellow dads would have about race.

But life is complicated! It's a lot to ask for a dad to think critically about all this the moment they first hold their child.

So let's not wait until our children are born. Let's begin the work before they are born, so when they ask those tough questions, we've done our homework.

SHIFTING FROM ALLY TO ADVOCATE

UNPACKING PRIVILEGE

In the previous chapter, we talked about how we must educate ourselves before we can take action. Now let's see how we can implement change.

In 1989, Dr. Kimberle Crenshaw coined the phrase "intersectionality" to explore how our complex identities impact our experiences. It began in a law class where students were arguing about the impact of western culture on women. Dr. Crenshaw explained all women were impacted by their gender, but certain women, specifically Black women, face additional hardships based on the color of their skin.

Crenshaw built this theory within the context of the legal system, but it has since grown within diversity and inclusion spaces. Began on legal processes, the impact of the phrase has grown in our culture. And as a man, who's White, Heterosexual, and Cisgender (meaning my sexual identity and gender identity align), I face relatively few challenges to my experience. Yet far too often, the perceived threats to people who look like me are seen as actual threats because they attack the social order that keeps us at the top.

And as a father, it is my belief that I have an obligation to engage in those hardships so I can dismantle them for my children. This process can take many forms and many theorists have created models for how individuals can become advocates for change. But the basic structure looks like this.

- The Personal Level, or the internal work we have to do with ourselves.
- The Interpersonal Level, or how we engage with our closest family and friends.
- The Systems Level, or how we recognize the larger cultural influence and systems that maintain a semblance of order.

As you might expect, the systems level is where we see the biggest challenges, but as the late Archbishop Desmond Tutu often reminded us, "I am because you are." Our existence is bound together and for all of us to succeed, we must engage in change together.

THE INTERCULTURAL DEVELOPMENT INVENTORY
The process of becoming antiracist, or an advocate for systems that dismantle racist practices, we need to shift our mindset. This is easier said than done, but the Intercultural Development Inventory breaks this process into five parts.

While I had heard of this inventory, my friends at the *DadGenes* podcast, Harris K Tay, Bryan Jackson, and Dedan Bruner, made it a reality. Their podcast explores the intersections of fatherhood and race. I highly recommend listening to their two seasons.

The goal with the IDI is to move you along a continuum from being unaware of the problems in society, and in fact, denying those problems exist, to a place where you see the interconnectedness of the cultures that exist in our country. Through five stages, individuals move from denial to polarization to minimization to acceptance and adaptation. For the sake of simplicity, I'll focus on racial awareness and my journey.

Growing up in Indiana, I didn't have a classmate who wasn't white until I was in seventh grade. There were plenty of people of color in my hometown, in my church, and in other spaces I frequented, but when it came to the classroom, 99 percent of my early education was not very diverse. Our teachers taught about racism by celebrating Martin Luther King Jr.

As a child, I wasn't in denial as much as living in ignorance of the harmful effects of racism. By the time I reached high school, my class had more diversity and representation, but also plenty of white supremacy with Confederate flags and worse flying around. Instead of standing up for those minority voices and victims of patriarchal and racist structures, my mind asked why people wouldn't conform and adapt to the way things were. I would place judgment on those victimized by our culture rather than those perpetrating the violence.

If I wasn't asking why people weren't conforming, I was minimizing the difference and rationalizing the differences away by looking at those within the minority communities who had adapted and thrived.

In college, the shift in my mindset came through engaging with classmates in my world religion courses. Through the study of Judaism, Islam, and Buddhism, I saw the importance of other worldview and appreciated them for their contributions, but I still saw them as separate and disconnected from my own experiences.

Then, after college, when I moved to Anchorage for a year of service through the Jesuit Volunteer Corps, I began making connections. In the beginning, I was set on "saving the world" and being a champion for homeless issues. In all the hubris of a twenty-three-year-old with a bachelor's degree, I stepped into my role thinking I could make systemic changes without understanding the cultures and systems I stepped into.

Then one day, a client came into my office. I turned to him and smiled and asked, "What can I do for you today?"

His name was Simon and he had grown up in Gambell, a bush village in the northwestern corner of Alaska. His home was closer to Russian mainland than the US and had come to Anchorage because he needed a medical procedure. When we had first met a few weeks earlier, he told me he had never seen a paved road or traffic light. Then he fell into a crowd that introduced him to drugs and alcohol, and he got stuck.

On this day, something wasn't right with him. His eyes were shifty and his face muscles slack. Technically, by rule, no one was allowed into the building if they were intoxicated, but when it was negative twenty degrees, we made plenty of exceptions for safety reasons.

"What the fuck do you know?" he shouted.

"Excuse me?" I reacted and looked past him to the monitors. They were already walking toward us.

"You come here and say you want to help me, but you don't know me. You don't know the shit I've seen. Fuck you."

Before I could say anything else, they ushered him out of the building. Mac, the head monitor, checked on me and I said I was fine. But I wasn't.

I had considered Simon one of my trusted clients in the shelter. He would share details with me about relationships, who was on what drug, and how many times the veterans had been through rehab at the V.A. hospital. I had never expected him to react so strongly to me and in such a negative way.

ADVOCACY MEANS SOLIDARITY

That night, I spoke with my housemates about it. And I realized that my job wasn't to save anyone. It was to see them as people and care for them and advocate for them so conditions for people experiencing homelessness would improve. I couldn't do that if I didn't understand

and appreciate their stories and experiences or the cultures from which they came.

Thus, for the remainder of the year, I stopped thinking about how I could save the world, but how I could understand it and be a part of it.

I started seeing similarities and bridges between my Midwest Catholic upbringing and a Native Alaskan raised on a small island in the middle of the Bering Sea.

This knowledge and awakening would carry with me through graduate school into my work as an interfaith campus minister. Long before I had children, I worked with students to build bridges across lines of religious differences and to help them see their similarities were far more important than their differences.

This same knowledge informed my conversation with my daughter as we continued walking through the forest. And continues to appear in conversations with dads.

While recruiting dads to be interviewed, I reached out to a former supervisor. He agreed to be interviewed. Tim is an imposing man, standing over six feet tall. He's also got a black belt in karate and has the physique you'd find in a superhero movie. Not only that, but he's also got a raspy deep voice, which he rarely uses because if he is upset, all he has to do is stare you down.

Needless to say, he scared the shit out of me when I was a graduate assistant in his office. But now, he smiles and laughs and treats me like an equal. So when I asked him how he was going to prepare for fatherhood, I was surprised by how serious he got.

"Honestly, I didn't do much. I didn't read any books because I knew they wouldn't have what I needed. My goal was to raise my daughter to be the counter narrative of all that society would tell her to be."

"What does counter narrative mean?"

"My daughter is going to be overly sexualized. As a girl who presents as Black, people will assume she'll live off the welfare state and not care about school. But let me tell you something, Brian. When she was five, she asked about segregation. I would have preferred she ask me where babies come from."

We shared a laugh, betraying the serious tone of the conversation.

Tim isn't alone in his concerns for his child. Other men of color I spoke with had similar stories and experiences. Those with sons are preparing for "the Talk." Not the birds and the bees, but the one where they educate their children about how to not be shot by the police and how to find the balance between polite and firm.

But what these fathers are also doing is building community to advocate for change. If one person takes a risk, they will fail and fall all alone. If everyone takes a risk, then society changes. These fathers are striving to do that.

Another dad, Bryan, tells me how he will drive ninety minutes to ensure his kids see a Black Santa. Living in the suburbs of Washington, DC, means they have hours of traffic to reach the one mall that advertised they'd have Black Santa, but he didn't care. He was going to make it there because representation matters, and his kids need to see themselves in their heroes.

But Bryan's road to fatherhood wasn't easy.

"When people ask me what it was like to become a dad, I always ask, which time?" Bryan smiled at his response to my first question.

"Why is that?" I replied.

"Because my wife and I endured three miscarriages before Sam came into our life." Bryan paused for a moment and continued, "As we progressed through the pregnancy with Sam, each doctor's visit brought me a little closer to hope, but I could never feel really excited. I could never allow myself to relax because there were three other children who I never got to meet. But, when I got to hold Sam in my arms, I finally let myself think of myself as a dad. And now that I am a dad, two times over, I'm doing everything I can to make the world a better place for them."

As a Black man married to an Asian woman, Bryan constantly assesses how to educate his children to keep them safe and to find role models for them. When his kids go to sleepovers, he calls their friends' parents to ensure the space is safe. He built a community called AttachMENt before connecting with Dedan to start *DadGenes* because of his passion for the topic.

NEXT STEPS

As I referenced earlier, in *Hunt, Gather, Parent*, Doucleff points out how the humans survived for thousands of years without modern Western thinking. Those parents cared for their children and protected them from harsh environments. They must have been doing something right in their strategies for protecting their children and keeping their families and communities safe.

With modern technology, medicine, and systems that have the power to keep us much safer than our ancestors, the new challenges are within the social norms and cultures. These norms and cultures will be constantly challenged by our children because we pushed back and challenged our parents, too.

So we have a choice. Do we continue to live in a world where our children will have to hide their identities and dreams, or do we work to change the world?

I prefer to change the world in whatever small ways I can. Thankfully, I've built a community to hold me accountable and work toward equity. The power of this community, and how to find your own community to do the same work, will be covered in the next chapter.

PART 6

COMMUNITY

13

FINDING YOUR COMMUNITY

"I'm not a part of many groups, but talking to other dads here has given me confidence in my abilities to connect with my kids."

—SIMON M.

After I graduated from Butler University, I moved to Anchorage, Alaska, to serve a year with the Jesuit Volunteer Corps. I had a job at a homeless shelter helping people gain access to housing, medical needs, and sometimes just a hand to hold when they were at the end of their rope. I ended up working there for nearly four years. Then, in the spring 2007, I decided to leave for graduate school. The night before I was to leave, I got cold feet. Sitting in Chumley's bar, my friend Sarah talked some sense into me.

"What if I don't make any friends?" I asked.

"Brian, be serious. Did you know anyone when you came to Anchorage?" Sarah asked indignantly.

"No," I admitted.

"And over the course of four years, did you not build a community of friends?"

"Yes."

"So what makes you think you won't do it again?" She took a swig of her beer and put it down in victory. I smiled across our booth and toasted to her victory. But she wasn't finished.

"Brian, you can't not make community around you. Recognize your gift and just know that all of us will be cheering you on."

The next morning, my cousin and dad would drive with me for four days from Anchorage down to Seattle, where I would start graduate school.

I would indeed create new communities with my graduate cohort before moving on to Milwaukee and finally in Chicago. I don't know if I ever would have imagined Evanston would be my adult home after living in so many places, but I met my wife, who made it very clear Chicago was her home. We compromised on Evanston so that I could have a yard.

In all those places, I built community, made long-lasting friendships, and learned more about the human spirit than I thought possible. And if you asked any of those friends if they saw me co-founding a non-profit organization grounded in community, none of them would be surprised.

THE IMPACT OF OUR VIRTUAL COMMUNITY

As I mentioned in chapter one, I had no clue what Chris and I created would become a global community. Nor could any of us predict the COVID-19 pandemic. As the old Yiddish adage goes, "Man makes plans, and God laughs." So Chris and I learned to be flexible and meet the demands that arose during the pandemic's height.

Instead of launching local chapters based on members in our Facebook group, we doubled down on the virtual space. We began highlighting different members each week. We partnered with Dove to focus on healthy body image in our daughters for a month-long campaign. Based on the reactions and conversations we had with members, we, as dads, have just as many self-esteem issues as our tween and teen daughters. And most of us hadn't realized how much our negative self-talk was affecting them.

We held our first dad-daughter virtual dance the summer of 2020. One of our members was a DJ and he reached out with the idea. So we ran with it. Hundreds of dads watched the livestream and posted photos dancing in their kitchens and living rooms. I wore a suit, and my daughters wore Disney princess dresses. We would have loved to dance in person with our friends, but given the state of the world, we still made do.

Our group wasn't just for moments of joy. Members regularly posted cries for help. Early in its formation, a dad from Utah made a post telling all of us his child was better off without him. Within minutes of the post going live, we had dads direct messaging Chris and me, asking if they could do anything to help him. Others were contacting local authorities to get an officer to show up to do a wellness check. One of those first responders would later become our first board president.

Because of that experience, we all recognize the power this community had. We all recognized we had built something truly unique. A space where men felt they could be honest and raw and vulnerable. A place where they could get honest feedback and support, but also accountability and a dose of tough love when they needed it.

As the pandemic raged on, it became abundantly clear that dads need community just like everyone else. And if any dad tells you otherwise, they are kidding themselves. As I mentioned earlier, the lone wolf isn't something to idolize.

THE IMPORTANCE OF COMMUNITY
In writing this book, I found hundreds of research articles that highlight the power of our social bonds and social structures that underscore the need for our communities. One specific researcher, John Cacioppo, has dedicated his life to the study of loneliness and his findings are critical influences on our strategy.

His book, *Loneliness*, covers a lot of ground, but I want to present two key takeaways. The first is being alone and being lonely are not the same and community shouldn't force members to engage past the point of discomfort. We all need space to ourselves to be able to do the deep work I describe in chapter four.

Cacioppo points out that you can still feel very lonely while being in a crowd and engaging with people. In this way, a community does not exist solely to please its figurehead. If that's the case, you've got a cult of personality, not a true community. When "Dads with Daughters" started to expand rapidly, I was adamant that Chris and I not be seen as the only experts. Hundreds of coaches and parenting experts were in the group just as there were plenty of mechanics, lawyers, and stay-at-home dads. Whenever possible, we invited people to share their gifts and talents and offer their support to one another.

This strategy led to our virtual dad-daughter dance, a member doing weekly health presentations during the early days of the pandemic, and eventually our monthly DadChat conversations. It also led to our "Dad of the Week" campaign to have a three-month waitlist with dads eager to share their stories.

The second takeaway from Cacioppo's work: as social creatures, we seek support no matter the circumstances. In a classic study with rhesus monkeys, scientists put baby monkeys in a cage with a wireframe model of a mother and a soft furry model. Within the wireframe model, the scientists put a spout for the monkey to get milk.

Throughout the experiment, the baby monkey would cling to the soft mold and transfer to the wire frame to drink only to return to the soft furry model again.

In speaking with dads, many told me their parents didn't emphasize how to build those social connections past their childhood. As stated before, men are taught to be protectors and shun emotion, not build communities where emotions are open and discussed.

Yet, we need to be able to build relationships and lean on those relationships when times are tough. We've seen it time and again within the group with those posts crying for help. But again, a post is a quick connection that is easily lost to the algorithm and flow of information. The deeper connections have happened in the message threads and virtual conversations. They've happened in the in-person meetups that occur when dads realize they live near one another but without the virtual "Dads with Daughters" community, they would have never known it.

The biggest lesson from my time in Anchorage, Alaska, was when you set out to save someone, you learn a lot more about yourself and your abilities. Simon, whom I mentioned in the previous chapter, gave me that lesson, and I've kept it with me through every job and community I've helped to create. When we developed the policies and guidelines for the Dads with Daughters group, I made sure I wasn't leading from a place of authority. Instead, I told my team we had to approach the group from a place of collegiality, equity, and respect.

And of course, as you might expect, we still made plenty of mistakes, but out of this latest experience, four values arose.

COMMUNITIES SAVE

The first is Support. Dads need a community to find support and find commonalities with others who are on the journey of fatherhood. None of our journeys are identical. But as I've watched dads join, post, and comment online or sit around a table at a bar with a beer in hand, the common threads of joy and challenge emerge.

One father, Devin, became "viral" within our group when he posted a request for prayers. His daughter was going through chemotherapy, and he had just lost his job. We have a policy of not allowing fundraisers, but the outpouring of messages and support drove us to allow an exception for all of us to provide him with financial and emotional support while his daughter was in the hospital. As of the time of this writing, his daughter is in remission and doing well.

The second is Accountability. In our community, we have plenty of dads who are striving to be the best they can be for their children, but sometimes we fall short. One weekend, I logged in to check my messages and noticed a young father's post. He was seeking guidance about a situation with his co-parent and child.

His post began: "My woman..." and continued with an excerpt from a text from her that demanded he be more participatory and attentive at home. She had recently moved out of their shared home and in with her mom because he had been spending too much time on video games. As a moderator team, we debated letting the post go live because we feared he might get ridiculed by others. But, we allowed the post because we knew he needed to hear from other dads and get some hard truths.

Within sixty minutes, the post received over two hundred comments. Several days later, there were close to four hundred, and we only had to remove a handful for inappropriate language. To our surprise, most of our members reminded the young dad to "be more attentive" and to "step it up" because "this is what fatherhood is." Our collective favorite came from an older dad, who simply stated, "You can begin by stop calling her 'my woman.'"

Most of these comments came from a place of love because we've all been there and sometimes we find ourselves back there again. We all have made mistakes early into our fatherhood journey and failed to realize how transformational fatherhood is. Thankfully, the young man remained in the group, and I even saw him post a reply thanking the older dad.

Third is Vulnerability. Far too often, we see vulnerability as a weakness. As men, we are taught to be strong and tough and resilient, and vulnerability appears to be the opposite of all these things. In leadership development, many ascribe to Gallup's Strength-Based approach that we should focus on our strengths and not our weaknesses. However, to know our weaknesses and to be open to explore our faults is critical for our growth as well.

One father I spoke with for this book shared his child was conceived through in vitro fertilization. I thanked him for sharing, and he continued to share that it had been his sperm count that was the issue, not his wife's eggs. When the doctor told them this, he struggled with the news. He'd been raised on the belief that his manhood was tied to his virility. To have that virility taken away was not something in his plan. Like Phil and me, he searched for a community to process this news, but found relatively little.

This brings us to the last value: Equity. Equity takes many forms, but at its core, equity is a process that creates an opportunity for everyone to have a part in the process. In the home, it can look like using Eve Rodsky's method of Fair Play to open communication lines and connection. In the workplace, it can look like opportunities for those who have been silenced to take leadership roles and influence workplace culture. In our community, within the context of the first three values, it looks like using our experiences and places of power to open up opportunities for our children to grow and take action.

For Fathering Together, we stood upon this value when we organized our first publication called "Fathering Stories." It is a collection of stories from our members, much like the live storytelling nights I first organized. Simran Jeet Singh authored one of our chapters.

Simran Jeet Singh is a scholar, anti-Islamophobia activist, and Director at the Aspen Institute. He's also a dad of two daughters who love listening to NPR. I could hear it in the background when we spoke on the phone for his interview. His recent children's book, *Fauna Singh Keeps Going*, was inspired by an interaction he had with his daughter.

Simran picked his daughter up from preschool and she said, "Dad, none of our picture books have people like me in them."

Her lament came as little surprise to Simran. There aren't many books with Sikh children on our bookshelves in the United States. Simran wasn't one to let his daughter's sorrow last, so he set to work recounting Fauja Singh's biography. While Fauja's story is incredible, and I highly recommend you look him up, the main point for Simran and his daughter was to increase representation of Sikhs in our cultural landscape.

When the book came out, Simran showed his daughter, and she screamed with delight. "Dad, they look like me!"

THE FRATERNITY OF DAD COMMUNITIES

These values are not unique to Fathering Together. As Fathering Together has taken shape, we've done so in community with other dad communities and initiatives.

Ten years ago, Doug French and John Pacini launched the Dad 2.0 Summit. Its purpose was to bring together dad bloggers and influencers to grow their businesses and social media strategies. My co-founder, Chris Lewis, has been an integral part of its growth and social media presence and has told me numerous times that the community that has grown around the annual conference pushed him to be a stronger and more connected dad.

Similarly, Sergio Rosario Diaz and his Soy Super Papa community has only grown tighter throughout the pandemic because of these values. Sergio's commitment to supporting Latino fathers throughout the Americas has offered support and opportunities to hold fathers accountable to their responsibilities within the context of machismo culture.

Finally, there is the City Dads Group powered by Matt Schneider and Larry Schoenfeld. Like so many dads I've mentioned, they met and forged a group of new dads in New York City by organizing meetups in the city parks. Twenty years later and spanning nearly three dozen locations, their dad-child activity-based programs and meetups have helped thousands of dads to find support and accountability while providing space for vulnerability and bringing about equity for all.

YOUR FAMILY IS COMMUNITY

In the introduction, I told the story of my daughter yelling at me for not being present. The real lesson was the harsh reminder I'd turned my back on the most important community of my life: my family. When we pour ourselves into work, when we pour ourselves into our hobbies and other interests, what we are really doing is robbing our families of our gifts.

Most dads I work with make the rationalization they are working long hours so their families are well off. However, the adage comes to mind that when we reach our deathbed, no one talks about the deals they closed or the deadlines they missed. They talk about the missed opportunities they have with their kids.

So don't forget your family is your most important community. Your kids won't.

CONCLUSION

When I was thirteen, my history teacher gave my class the assignment to interview a living ancestor. I chose my maternal grandfather. I'd only heard sporadic stories from my mom, aunts, and uncles. I hadn't yet grown closer to him in my adulthood. So he drove down to visit, and we set up at our dining room table for the interview.

He shared with me stories of attending a school in rural Indiana with only ten classmates and riding the school bus his father drove. He shared stories of milking cows, harvesting corn, and enlisting in the military during World War II. I pressed on beyond childhood and asked him about becoming a dad for the first time.

"Grandpa, what was it like becoming a dad?" I asked.

He burst out laughing, and I noticed his eyes were tearing up. From the kitchen, my dad laughed and shouted, "Brian, you have no clue what you are asking!"

Instead of answering, my grandfather pulled me toward him into a bear hug and kept laughing. He never answered what it was like. He just told me how he missed getting to the hospital because he got stuck behind a train. He arrived two hours after his son was born.

Now that I'm a dad, I realize the hug was his actual answer. Becoming a father is to hold on to our kids as long as possible before relinquishing them to the trials of adulthood and (maybe) parenthood. It's being present and available when a hug is needed most, even if we aren't asking for one. It's recognizing we won't ever be perfect, but that our imperfections help our children to learn to navigate the world around them far better than if we did everything perfectly for them.

My grandfather wasn't perfect. He had a temper, and he wasn't always politically correct in his understandings of the world. But one thing he did best was love each of us and accept us through our good and bad decisions.

In the previous pages, I've shared personal stories from dads who have journeyed these last four years of fatherhood with me. Few of us have all the answers, but all of us have dedicated ourselves to finding strength and living into our servant leadership. I hope you've learned something from this book. I hope at least one chapter gives you strategies to deepen your relationships with your children and walk through life with a dad-first mindset.

And if I've missed an answer, please join Fathering Together and lend your voice. Our goal is to continue to expand the definitions of fatherhood and what makes up a dad. Without your voice, we won't ever completely understand fatherhood. So reach out, and I promise you won't be sorry for it.

And last but not least, here's the TL;DR version that I didn't put at the start, but wanted to include anyway!

PRE-WORK

- Recognize you will never be perfect.
- Do some deep psychological and spiritual work. Don't just make the crib when you are expecting a baby.

COMMUNICATION

- Be emotionally courageous. You have it in you to express more than happiness, sadness, and anger.
- Listen. As you were probably told by your parents, you were given one mouth and two ears for a reason.
- Communicate and use words when necessary. Our kids pick up on everything we do and say. The emphasis is on the "do" though. You may share all the life lessons in the world, but if they see you smoking and eating Twinkies, chances are they won't grow up to be a health and fitness instructor.
- Be present. Don't just show up for the highlights. Show up when it's boring and tedious. Play with Barbies, build Lego castles, and throw a ball until your arms hurt.

OTHER-ORIENTED

- Be accepting. You will want so much for your children, but remember they have their own vision and identity. Accept them for who they are.

- Remember we belong to each other. There is a Zulu phrase called *Ubuntu*. Multiple translations exist, but the most common was written by Rev. Desmond Tutu when he said, "My humanity is bound up with yours. That goes for you and your kids, you and your partner, you and everyone. Act accordingly."

ADVOCACY

- Be a lifelong learner. Paulo Freire, in *Pedagogy of the Oppressed*, wrote about the importance of teachers learning from their students. The same is true for parents. In almost every social revolution, it came from children and youth and helped to redefine values and culture. Don't close your mind to the opportunities this change will bring for you.
- Advocate for them. No matter how your kid identifies, they deserve every opportunity to thrive. It's in the Declaration of Independence... they wrote it as the pursuit of happiness, but you could argue that it's the same thing.

COMMUNITY

- Be in, within, and of community. We are social beings. If we can't live together, we'll die alone.

There is an old proverb of mixed origin that states, "It takes a village to raise a child," but as my friend Craig shared with me in his interview, "It takes a village to be a good dad too." You'll find you're a better dad for it and your kids will appreciate the terrible dad jokes you pick up from your peers too!

ACKNOWLEDGMENTS

First and foremost, thank you to my wife, Laura, and my daughters, Clara and Natalie for enriching my life.

Thank you to my parents Chuck and Lucia, and all my other "parents:" Rena and Ross Aiken, Sharon and Bruce Graves, Mary Ann and Terry Lucterhand, Kevin and Susan Neal who helped define what healthy parenthood can be.

Thank you to my fellow dads, especially my Facebook team: Mike, Tim, Dave, Dave, Josh, Bradley, Ivan, Joseph, as well as my Evanston crew: Thom, Dean, Jantzen, David, Aaron, Adrian, Michael, Michael, Joe, and Luke.

Thanks to my Movie Club: BMac, Swan Princess, Skinny D, Shipley, Fergs, Gromski, and Uncle Cheese.

Thank you to my fellow gender equity advocates who push me to dig deeper and uncover more of myself in this work: Aaron, Jessica, Molly, Tara, Miriam, Eve, Blessing, Kate, Gayatri, Tami, Sarah, Tet, and Jett.

Thank you to Chris for being with me from day one. Thank you to John for helping us develop our education strategy. Thanks to Tim for giving us a voice. Thank you to my current and past board members for honing our vision: Emily, Thom, Michelle, Mel, Sehreen, Ehime, David, Robert, Tee, Dai, and Lawrence.

Thank you to New Degree Press, especially Eric Koester, Alexander Pyle, and Chuck Oexmann for making this book a reality.

And finally, thank you to everyone who pre-ordered the book and to my beta readers (Keith, Aaron, Jett, Kate, and Sean) for your faith in this journey: Aaron Cohen, Aaron Pina, Adrian Esquivel, Allen Carter, Amber Hacker, Amy J Henderson, Andrew Greenia, Anna Marie Johnson Teague, Anne Downey, Antoine Johnson, Ashley Singla, Audrey Lucterhand, Bailey Gordon, Ben Correia-Hacker, Becca Cacayuran, Ben Killoy, Billy Korinko, Blessing Adesiyan, Brian Houze, Brian McCammack, Bridget Turner Kelly, Bruce Linton, Bryan & Amy Malone, Carolyn Woo & Dave Bartkus, Chris Foley, Chris Murphy, Christopher Lewis, Colleen Harvey, Connie Meyer, Cordan Haveron, Craig Ferguson, Craig Steven Parks, Dan McDowell, Daniel Mercer, Daniel Weber, David Clark, David Smith, Dean Radcliffe,Dennis Remke, Drew Vriesman, Ed Frauenheim, Elliot Haspel, Eileen Downey, Elizabeth Conrath, Eric Koester, Evan Newton, Eve Rodsky, Gretchen Schneider, Harris Tay, Jacob Greenstein, Jaime Baim Hansen, Jake Edling, James Mahoehney, Janine Berridge, Jantzen Loza, Jason Dietz, Jason Gromski, Jason Hacker, Jeff Schmidt, Jeremy Roadruck, Jessica Cabral, Jessica DeGroot, Jett

Stone, Jim Young, John Gleason, John Lietzau, John Millner, John Shusterich, John Yurcisin, Jonathan B Crozier, Joseph Monical, Joseph Saucedo, Justin Knoy, Kate Drane, Kathryn Mangino, Keith Edwards, Kelly Benkert, Kent H Frazier, Kevin Gruenberg, Kevin O'Connell, Kimberly Wolf, Kristin Rubbelke, LaNysha Adams, Ph.D., Laura Bomkamp, Laura Smiley, Leslie Forde, Leslie Skaistis, Linda Dearman, Lori Mihalich-Levin, Lucia Anderson, Lucy Gillespie, Luke Chitwood, Mara Siler-Price, Marcos Gonzales, Mark Greene, Mary Arth, Mary Beth Ferrante, Maryann Lucterhand, Michael Andersen-Leavey, Michael Kendricks, Michael Miro, Michelle Travis, Mike Zeller, Miriam Williams, Molly Robertshaw, Nathan Goldberg, Nathan Shipley, Patrick Downey, Paul Baron, Peter Merkel, Phil Hanson, Philip Mott, Rachel Lucterhand, Sam Goodman, Samuel Tepper, Sarah Johal, Shannon Copp, Sean Harvey, Shannon Milligan, Sharon Moore, Sheehan David Fisher, Stephenie Chaudoir, Steven Sundstrom, Susan & Dick Carpenter, Ted Gonder, Thomas Walstrum, Tim Cigelske, Tom Ferrell, Tommy Maloney, Tony Stark Policci, Trent Carlson, Tuseef Chaudhry, and Zachary Gerdes.

APPENDIX A: SOURCES

INTRODUCTION

Brooks, David. "David Brooks: The Nuclear Family Was a Mistake." *The Atlantic.* 11 Feb. 2022, www.theatlantic.com/magazine/archive/2020/03/the-nuclear-family-was-a-mistake/605536.

Greenleaf, Robert. *SERVANT AS LEADER ESSAY (Rev Edition).* Westfield, IN: The Greenleaf Center for Servant Leadership, 2022.

CHAPTER 2: WHO DADS HAVE BEEN

Doucleff, Michaeleen. *Hunt, Gather, Parent: What Ancient Cultures Can Teach Us About the Lost Art of Raising Happy, Helpful Little Humans.* New York: Avid Reader Press, Simon and Schuster, 2022.

Hooks, Bell. *The Will to Change: Men, Masculinity, and Love.* 1st ed. New York: Washington Square Press, 2004.

Kraemer, Sebastian. "The Origins of Fatherhood: An Ancient Family Process." Family Process, vol. 30, no. 4, 1991, pp. 377–92. https://doi.org/10.1111/j.1545-5300.1991.00377.x.

Linton, Bruce. *Fatherhood: The Journey from Man to Dad. 1st ed.* Pennsauken Township, NJ: BookBaby, 2017.

Livingston, Gretchen, and Kim Parker. "8 Facts about American Dads." 30 May 2020. www.pewresearch.org/fact-tank/2019/06/12/fathers-day-facts.

Samuel, Lawrence. *American Fatherhood: A Cultural History.* Lanham, MD: Rowman and Littlefield Publishers, 2015.

Swan, Jonathan. "A Cultural History of Fatherhood and Its Retrieval." 8 June 2021. cbmw.org/2021/06/08/a-cultural-history-of-fatherhood-its-retrieval.

CHAPTER 3: WHO DADS CAN BE

Bjarki. "7 Time Consuming Things an Average Joe Spends on in a Lifetime." *Tempo.* 23 Nov. 2021. www.tempo.io/blog/7-time-consuming-things-an-average-joe-spends-in-a-lifetime.

Cox, Josie. "Paternity Leave: The Hidden Barriers Keeping Men at Work."12 July 2021. www.bbc.com/worklife/article/20210712-paternity-leave-the-hidden-barriers-keeping-men-at-work.

Frauenheim, Ed and Edward M. Adams. *Reinventing Masculinity: The Liberating Power of Compassion and Connection.* Oakland, CA: Berrett-Koehler Publishers, 2020.

Hare, Brian, and Vanessa Woods. *Survival of the Friendliest: Understanding Our Origins and Rediscovering Our Common Humanity.* NewYork: Random House Trade Paperbacks, 2021.

Harvard Business School. "The Caring Company."Accessed 27 June 2022. www.hbs.edu/managing-the-future-of-work/research/Pages/the-caring-company.aspx.

Jared, Diamond. *Guns, Germs, and Steel: The Fates of Human Societies. 20th Anniversary.* New York: W. W. Norton and Company, 2017.

Petts, Richard J., et al. "A Gendered Pandemic: Childcare, Homeschooling, and Parents' Employment during COVID-19." Gender, Work & Organization, vol. 28, no. S2, 2021, pp. 515–34. https://doi.org/10.1111/gwao.12614.

CHAPTER 4: WE'RE NOT PERFECT

Hewitt, Paul L. "Perfecting, Belonging, and Repairing: A Dynamic-Relational Approach to Perfectionism." Canadian Psychology/Psychologie Canadienne, vol. 61, no. 2, 2020, pp. 101–10. https://doi.org/10.1037/cap0000209.

"Spanx Founder Sara Blakely Learned an Important Lesson about Failure from Her Dad — Now She's Passing It on to Her 4 Kids." *Business Insider.* 17 June 2018. www.businessinsider.com/spanx-founder-sara-blakely-redefine-failure-2016-10?international=true&r=US&IR=T.

CHAPTER 5: DOING THE DEEP WORK

National Institute of Mental Health (NIMH). "Major Depression." Accessed 27 June 2022. www.nimh.nih.gov/health/statistics/major-depression.

CHAPTER 6: BEING PRESENT

Schafer, Jack and Marvin Karlins. *The Like Switch: An Ex-FBI Agent's Guide to Influencing, Attracting, and Winning People Over.* New York: Atria Books, 2015.

CHAPTER 7: BEING EMOTIONALLY COURAGEOUS

Johns Hopkins Medicine. "Twin-to-Twin Transfusion Syndrome (TTTS)." 8 Aug. 2021. www.hopkinsmedicine.org/health/conditions-and-diseases/twintotwin-transfusion-syndrome-ttts#:%7E:text=Twin%2Dto%2Dtwin%20transfusion%20syndrome%20(TTTS)%20is%20a,for%20development%20in%20the%20womb.

Zaki, Jamil. *The War for Kindness: Building Empathy in a Fractured World.* New York: Crown, 2020.

CHAPTER 8: COMMUNICATING AND USE WORDS WHEN NECESSARY

Doucleff, Michaeleen. *Hunt, Gather, Parent: What Ancient Cultures Can Teach Us About the Lost Art of Raising Happy, Helpful Little Humans.* New York: Avid Reader Press, Simon and Schuster, 2022.

Dunstan Baby Language. "Dunstan Baby Language." 16 June 2022. www.dunstanbaby.com.

Rodsky, Eve. *Fair Play: A Game-Changing Solution for When You Have Too Much to Do (and More Life to Live).* London, England: Penguin Publishing Group, 2021.

CHAPTER 9: ACCEPTING YOUR KIDS (AND YOURSELF TOO!)

pflag. "Home." Accessed 29 Jun. 2022. https://pflag.org

thetrevorproject. "Home." Accessed 29 Jun. 2022. https://www.thetrevorproject.org/

CHAPTER 10: CULTIVATING A LEARNING MINDSET

Freire, Paulo, and Donaldo Macedo. *Pedagogy of the Oppressed: 50th Anniversary Edition. 4th ed.* London, England: Bloomsbury Academic, 2018.

CHAPTER 11: BECOMING AN ALLY

Adamick, Mike. *Raising Empowered Daughters: A Dad-to-Dad Guide.* New York: Seal Press, 2019.

Katz, Jackson. *The Macho Paradox.* Chicago: Sourcebooks Incorporated, 2019.

Kendi, Ibram. *How to Be an Antiracist.* London, England: One World, 2019.

Kivel, Paul. *Men's Work: How to Stop the Violence That Tears Our Lives Apart.* New York: Ballantine Books, 1995.

Rape, Abuse, and Incest National Network. "Statistics." Accessed 27 June 2022. www.rainn.org/statistics.

Roberts, Dorothy. *Fatal Invention: How Science, Politics, and Big Business Re-Create Race in the Twenty-First Century.* New York: The New Press, 2012.

Stack, Liam. "Light Sentence for Brock Turner in Stanford Rape Case Draws Outrage." *The New York Times.* 14 June 2016. www.nytimes.com/2016/06/07/us/outrage-in-stanford-rape-case-over-dueling-statements-of-victim-and-attackers-father.html.

UN Women Headquarters."Facts and Figures: Ending Violence against Women." Accessed 27 June 2022. www.unwomen.org/en/what-we-do/ending-violence-against-women/facts-and-figures.

CHAPTER 12: ADVOCATING FOR CHANGE

Crenshaw, Kimberlé. *On Intersectionality: Essential Writings.* New York: The New Press, 2023.

Intercultural Development Inventory. "Home." 21 May 2019. idiinventory.com.

Kendi, Ibram. *How to Be an Antiracist.* London, England: One World, 2019.

CHAPTER 13: FINDING YOUR COMMUNITY

Cacioppo, John, and William Patrick. *Loneliness: Human Nature and the Need for Social Connection.* New York: W. W. Norton and Company, 2009.

Singh, Simran Jeet, and Baljinder Kaur. *Fauja Singh Keeps Going: The True Story of the Oldest Person to Ever Run a Marathon.* New York: Kokila, 2020.

CONCLUSION

APPENDIX B: ORGANIZATIONS

FATHERING TOGETHER INFORMATION
- Fathering Together: https://www.fatheringtogether. org/
- Fatherhood Insider: https://fatherhood-insider.mn.co

AUSTRALIA
- The Fathering Project: https://thefatheringproject.org/
- Dads &: https://www.dads-and.com/

CANADA
- NextGenMen: https://www.nextgenmen.ca/
- Raising Humanity: https://raisinghumanity.com/

SOUTH AFRICA
- Sonke Gender Justice: https://genderjustice.org.za/

UNITED KINGDOM
- Music Football Fatherhood: https://musicfootballfatherhood.com/

UNITED STATES

- &Mother: https://andmother.org/
- A Call to Men: https://www.acalltomen.org/
- At Home Dad Network: https://athomedad.org/
- City Dad Group: https://citydadsgroup.com/
- Dad 2.0: https://dad2.com/
- Equimundo: https://www.equimundo.org/
- Fair Play: https://www.fairplaylife.com/
- Love-Dad: https://love-dad.org/
- Mindful Return: https://www.mindfulreturn.com/
- Mirza: https://www.heymirza.com/
- Oakland Men's Project: http://paulkivel.com/the-oakland-mens-project/
- Path Forward: https://www.pathforward.org/
- Soy Super Papa: https://www.instagram.com/soysuperpapa/?hl=en
- Superkin: https://superkin.com/